CW00554973

SCOTTISH REGION

Colour Album No 1

George C. O'Hara

Published by: CLYARD NOVELLA LIMITED
16 Garryhorn
Prestwick
South Ayrshire
Scotland KA9 2HU
Tel: 01292 479407

CLYARD NOVELLA LIMITED

Printed & bound by: Cambrian Printers Ltd,
Llanbadarn Road,
Aberystwyth,
Wales SY23 3TN

CAMBRIAN CP PRINTERS

Typesetting by Cambrian Printers Ltd

Colour separation and Reproduction by: Cambrian Printers Ltd

ISBN: 0-9530821-1-3

British Library Cataloguing in Publication Data.
A catalogue record for this book is available from the British Library.

CONTENTS

ACKNOWLEDGEMENTS

As an invaluable contribution towards the compilation of this book, the author is indebted to the following list of eminent railway photographers who took the photographs reproduced in this publication. This elite group of men were possessed with committed vision, patience and interest in recording pictorially the then insidiously changing and rapidly contracting entity that was the former British Railways, Scottish Region. Without their efforts this photographic record spanning nearly five decades of railway operation would not be possible, these photographers are: Douglas E. D. Blades, Dougald Cameron, Alan Carlaw, Roy M. Crombie, David M. Cross (Derek Cross), John Spencer Gilks, Roy Hamilton, Douglas Hume, Keith Jones (of the G.N.S.R.A.), Hugh Morton, Robin Nelson, Tom Noble, Ken Nuttall, Geo C. O'Hara, Douglas Paul, Ronnie Provan, Stuart Sellar, David C. Smith, W. A. C. Smith, George Norman Turnbull, Ron White (and the specific photographers of Colour-Rail).

Moreover this book recognises and appreciates the painstaking efforts of the thousands of former railway workers including management, staff and contractors who made the Scottish Region of British Railways perform amid the demoralising interference of political rationalisation that constantly changed the background and operating criteria throughout the entire duration of this nationalised company.

Furthermore the author thanks his wife Beatrice and their family for tolerating many lengthy and sometimes fruitless photographic expeditions throughout Scotland in attempts at capturing elusive traffic movements, some of which are depicted in this book, but others alas only remain compositions in the author's mind.

Additionally the author wishes to thank a small number of colleagues, whose oblique yet constructive comments subtly inspired certain elements of this book. Nevertheless, despite rendering such help, these few individuals expressed veiled embarrassment at being perceived as 'closet anoraks'! Unfortunately such reluctance with regard to personal recognition resulted in their identities not appearing on this page.

A capricious conversation with a fellow worker led to unexpected assistance with the task of proof reading and grammatically correcting the text. To this end sincere thanks are extended to Lynne Evans in recognition of her scholastic linguistic skills and her unabashed tolerance of the author's West of Scotland contorted vernacular.

GEORGE C. O'HARA.
Prestwick, January 2003

INTRODUCTION

This book is the first in what might become a series of photographic albums depicting the railways of Scotland in the era controlled by the former nationalised entity that was British Railways (Scottish Region), if a supply of material can be located to continue this format.

Covering a period that lasted nearly half a century, this book attempts to show a comprehensive record of erstwhile traditional railway operating scenes through its extensive arrangement of pictures in the following pages. Ranging from the smoke belching grime encrusted epoch of steam traction through several transitional phases of affordable modernisation up until the dawn of fragmented privatisation. The selection of illustrations depicted attempt to record the vast inventory of motive power, rolling stock, stations, yards, sheds, depots, real estate and variety of traffic, passengers and freight that comprised the business entirety of the fomer British Railways Scottish Region. No attempt was made to represent any of the twenty first century service companies with their gaudy kaleidescope of hi-tech rolling stock, text book theorised credo of push button control and operational wizardry that metamorphosed from the nationalised British Railways. The erstwhile railway network represented in this assemblage of photographs does not consist of any fun-fair colour schemes adorned with gimmick splattered acronyms.

Instead many work-worn locomotive, depots, stations, coaches, vans, wagons, yards and structures are shown conveying the traffic they were built to carry before conspiring governments sponsored 'out of gauge juggernauts', 'will o the wisp delivery vans', and inadequate revenue collection roadway schemes to hoover up what was left of rail borne commodities post the pruning and rationalisation period of the Beeching era.

This book has set out to cover as much of the former extensive B.R. Scottish Region network as the availability of suitable photographic material will allow. To this end the book has been set into 14 chapters which categorise specific elements of traditional railway operation, configuration, network and topography rather than a lengthy chronological potpourri of trains at work throughout the region. This format has enabled the author to provide several pictorial representations of lines and types of traffic that were previously poorly covered in other railway books.

Whilst a reference index of the locations depicted is provided, no attempt has been made to include maps or route diagrams. Despite the issue of copyright concerning the reproduction of maps, these types of publications are invariably accurate sources of reference in their own right, and as such make complimentary reading with regard to identification of the locations shown.

The author considers differentiation between types of motive traction on working railways is a cosmetic nicety that belies the reality of transitional modernisation, when early types of diesel and electric locomotives and multiple units shared the then extensive route network with various classes of steam engines.

Footnote: The publishers lament the inclusion of several dark and fuzzy illustrations in this compendium of erstwhile scenes of the former British Railways, Scottish Region. This decision to include these views of historical railway rarity outweighed the technical criticism for their exclusion.

Section 1

SELECTION OF SCOTTISH MAIN LINE SCENES AND RAILWAY TRAFFIC

This section of the book attempts to represent a selection of former railway scenes on some of the main line routes that existed under the aegis of British Railways Scottish Region. Because of the varying topography through which these lines ran, the range of scenery, type of passenger and freight carried and classes of traction and rolling stock varied considerably, as is envinced in the spread of photographs depicted in the following pages.

Ex LMSR Crab 2-6-0 #42908 leaks through Dalbeattie station in the Spring of 1964 with a mixed goods train from Stranraer to Dumfries.

Roy Hamilton

Ex LMSR Class 5 4-6-0 #45471 near Gatehouse of Fleet with a featherweight Saturday morning Dumfries to Stranraer goods train in May 1965. This sparse traffic comprising a vacuum fitted tube wagon and a brake van reflected the fact the line would close one month later.

Roy Hamilton

Ex LMSR Class 5 4-6-0 #45432 leaves Crossmichael with a Stranraer Town to Dumfries passenger working in May 1965.

Roy Hamilton

Ex LMSR Class 5 4-6-0 #45362 passes through the then still open station at Gretna Green with a mixed up goods train on the GSWR main line in July 1962. Note the rake of plate wagons in the adjacent sidings.

Roy M. Crombie

Ex LMSR rebuilt Royal Scot 4-6-0 #46167 "The Hertfordshire Regiment" rattles a lengthy rake of unfitted 16-ton mineral (coal) empties between Dalry and Kilmarnock on the GSWR line, bound for the then busy rail connected collieries of the Ayrshire coalfield in February 1963.

W. A. C. Smith

CLAYTON Class 17 Bo-Bo diesel electrics #'s D8542 & D8509 head a northbound mixed freight on the former GSWR main line through the then still open station at New Cumnock in the upper Nith Valley in April 1964.

D. C. Smith

E.E. Class 55 DELTIC #D.9010 recently named "Kings Own Scottish Borderer" leaves Dumfries and heads north up the GSWR main line after being named at Dumfries station in April 1965.

Robin Nelson

Ex LMSR Class 8f 2-8-0 #48321 heads a southbound train of steel ingots from one of the Colvilles Steel mills in Lanarkshire loaded in a rake of vacuum fitted boplate wagons presumably bound for rolling in an English mill or even for export. The consist is approaching Beattock station in July 1960. Note the still open for freight Beattock branch curving away to the right.

Roy M. Crombie

An Unidentified **E.E. Class 40 1 Co-Co 1 diesel electric** powers through Beattock station with a northbound "Royal Scot" train in June 1961. Note the steam trains waiting for access paths in Beattock sidings.

Roy M. Crombie

Ex LMSR Class 5 4-6-0 #45099 heads a southbound trainload of steel pipes loaded in a rake of bogie bolster wagons from the former Clydesdale tube mills of Stewarts & Lloyds at Mossend, Lanarkshire in June 1961. The train is seen near Crawford in the Clyde Valley.

R. M. Crombie

Ex LMSR DUCHESS Class 4-6-2 #46247 "City of Liverpool" looks every inch a thoroughbred Pacific loco, despite leaking some steam as she nears Beattock Summit with a north-bound express on a murky day in July 1962.

Roy M. Crombie

Ex LMSR DUCHESS Class 4-6-2 #46225 "Duchess of Gloucester" powers through Lamington in the Clyde Valley with a southbound express in August 1964, shortly before this class was debarred from hauling the crack Anglo-Scottish expresses.

Robin Nelson

A pair of unidentified **CLAYTON Class 17 Bo-Bo diesel electrics** glide towards Beattock Summit with an up mixed goods train in August 1969.

R. M. Crombie

Ex LNER A4 4-6-0 #60010 "DOMINION OF CANADA" pounds past Germiston Junction with a Glasgow Buchanan Street to Aberdeen express in August 1966.

Robin Nelson

Unidentified **N.B.L. Class 29 Bo-Bo diesel electric** emerges from Pinkston Tunnel into the throat of Glasgow Buchanan Street station with a train from Aberdeen in May 1966.

Roy M. Crombie

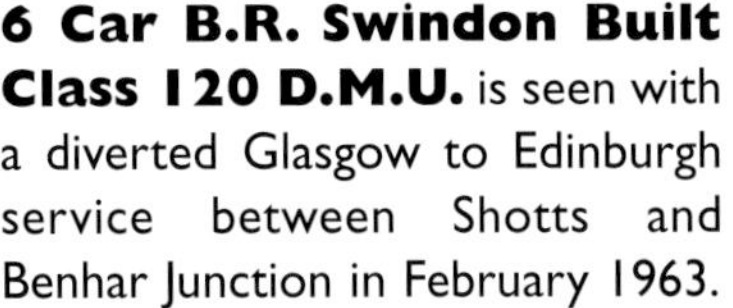

6 Car B.R. Swindon Built Class 120 D.M.U. is seen with a diverted Glasgow to Edinburgh service between Shotts and Benhar Junction in February 1963.

W. A. C. Smith

3 Car METRO CAMMELL Class 101 D.M.U. is seen climbing Balamanno Glen, near Glenfarg with a service from Perth to Edinburgh in April 1960.

R. M. Crombie

BRUSH Class 47 Co-Co diesel electric #D.1847 leaves Forfar with a morning express from Glasgow Buchanan Street to Aberdeen in July 1966. The recently closed locomotive shed (a sub-shed of Perth #63A) can be seen above the engine to the right.

Roy Hamilton

Recently Re-Engined and Reliveried **N.B.L. Class 29 Bo-Bo diesel electric #D6123** leaves Coupar Angus with a morning express from Glasgow Buchanan Street to Aberdeen in July 1967, the last year of operation of this service over the Strathmore Route.

Roy Hamilton

A frosty morning accentuates leaking steam from **Ex LNER V2 2-6-2 #60844** as it restarts a Perth to Aberdeen fitted mixed goods train south of Kinnaber Junction in April 1963.

Douglas Paul

Unidentified **E.C. Class 40 1 Co-Co 1 diesel electric** heads a lightweight eastbound train of D.C.L. 'whisky logo' vacuum fitted 35-ton bulk grain wagons at the site of the former Orbliston Junction between Inverness and Elgin in June 1970.

Roy M. Crombie

Unidentified **B.R.C.W. Class 27 Bo-Bo diesel electric** heads a lengthy Inverness to Mossend yard fitted freight south of Gleneagles in May 1978.

Tom H. Noble

Unidentified **B.R.C.W. Class 26 Bo-Bo diesel electric** with a short mixed goods train from Inverness to Kyle of Lochalsh is seen leaving picturesque Strathcarron with the distant mountains of Sheildaig beyond in June 1967.

Roy M. Crombie

E.E. Class 37 Co-Co #37.085 trundles the tiniest of payloads, a single 16-ton vacuum fitted coal wagon from Mossend yard to Oban through Glen Lochy in June 1983.

Tom H. Noble

Ex LMSR Class 5 4-6-0 #44968 climbs effortlessly through Coire Thain between Tyndrum Upper and Bridge of Orchy with a nicely mixed freight from Cadder Yard to Fort William in July 1961.

John Spencer Gilks

Sporting tablet catching recess, a feature of B.R. Scottish region locos, **E.E. Class 20 Bo-Bo diesel electric #D8130** lifts a Cadder yard to Fort William mixed freight towards the summit of Glenfalloch, near Crianlarich in May 1963.

Ken Nuttall

B.R.C.W. Class 27 Bo-Bo diesel electric #D5350 heads a mixed freight from Fort William to Cadder Yard south of Crianlarich in May 1963. Noticeable in the middle of the consist are four empty covhop wagons used to convey alumina from Burntisland to the Fort William British Aluminium Co. Ltd.

Ken Nuttall

Unidentified **B.R.C.W. Class 27 Bo-Bo diesel electric** heads a lengthy fitted freight from Cadder yard to Fort William away from Bridge of Orchy towards a picturesque mist shrouded Rannoch Moor in July 1974.

Tom H. Noble

Ex LNER D49 4-4-0 #62744 "THE HOLDERNESS" drifts down Borthwick Bank with a Carlisle to Millerhill mixed goods train on the Waverley Route in June 1960. The train consist comprises several empty 'blue spot' vacuum fitted fish vans being returned to various Scottish east coast fishing ports.

Roy M. Crombie

Ex LNER B.I. 4-6-0 #61349 rushes through a snowy Heriot station with a Waverley route stopping service in January 1966.

David C. Smith

A well patronised **GLOUCESTER Class 100 2-Coach D.M.U.** is seen near Eskbank with a Hawick-Edinburgh Waverley local in April 1966.

Geo. N. Turnbull

Comprising a lengthy rake of rusty unfitted 16-ton mineral wagons the Waverley Route track maintenance train is seen near Heriot hauled by an unidentified **B.R.C.W. Class 27 Bo-Bo diesel electric** in October 1967.

Geo. N. Turnbull

Unidentified **E.E. Class 40 1 Co-Co 1 diesel electric** approaches Fallahill Summit on the Waverley Route with an Edinburgh to Carlisle train in August 1968, comprising a rake of B.R. MK1 coaches in maroon and blue/grey liveries.

Geo. N. Turnbull

Section 2

SELECTION OF SCOTTISH BRANCH LINE SCENES AND RAILWAY TRAFFIC

This section of the book only manages to represent approximately 30% of the formerly extensive branch line network that once criss-crossed a large part of Scotland, especially the industrial lowlands. As virtually all of the branch lines and secondary routes were single track formations serving sparsely populated locations or specific industrial facilities, there is a photographic similarity in much of the traction and traffic shown in the following spread of pictures.

Unidentified **N.B.L. Class 21 Bo-Bo diesel electric** negotiates the tight curve out of Dufftown at Parkmore siding with an Elgin to Aberdeen via Craigellachie working in July 1966.

Roy Hamilton

B.R. SULZER Class 24 Bo-Bo diesel electric #D5070 passes the hamlet of Buckpool on the edge of Spey Bay with an afternoon Elgin-Aberdeen via Buckie working in July 1967.

Roy Hamilton

Unidentified **N.B.L. Class 21 Bo-Bo diesel electric** leaves Elgin and is seen near Lossie Junction with an afternoon train for Aberdeen via Buckie in June 1965.

Roy M. Crombie

N.B.L. Class 21 Bo-Bo diesel electric #D6140 passes the typical Moray Firth Fishing village of Portgordon with an afternoon local train from Buckie to Elgin in July 1967.

Roy Hamilton

The following three views are of the once busy Speyside goods train working in up and down directions (serving many famous distilleries) on different days in July 1966.

Unidentified **E.E. Class 20 Bo-Bo diesel electric** is seen in the typical Speyside woodland terrain between Carron and Aberlour with a lengthy nicely mixed goods working from Ballindalloch to Craigellachie.

Roy Hamilton

Unidentified **E.E. Class 20 Bo-Bo diesel electric** draws a lengthy trip freight comprising several D.C.L. bulk grain "whisky logo" wagons into Carron station, where an example of the B.R. standard vacuum fitted grain wagon is seen in a siding. This train is the northbound 10.10 Aviemore to Craigellachie goods service which ran until November 1968.

Roy Hamilton

Unidentified **E.E. Class 20 Bo-Bo diesel electric** nears Grantown-on-Spey East with an afternoon Craigellachie to Aviemore mixed trip freight. Up until closure of this route the railway carried virtually all of the raw materials used in the whisky industry as well as a proportion of the high-value world famous product.

D. C. Smith

Unidentified **B.R. STD Class 2 2-6-0** chuffs an afternoon Banff to Tillynaught Junction service away from Ladysbridge Halt in October 1963.

courtesy G.N.S.R.A. Collection

N.B.L. Class 21 Bo-Bo diesel electric #D6156 approaches Fraserburgh in a dull August day in 1963, where the stormy North Sea is pounding the shore in the background. The train is the morning goods working from Craiginches Yard, Aberdeen, comprising several empty 12-ton blue spot insul fish vans.

Roy M. Crombie

A CRAVENS Class 105 2-Car D.M.U. is seen amid the beauty of Royal Deeside near Cambus 'O' May with a late afternoon service from Ballater to Aberdeen in August 1963.

Roy M. Crombie

The following spread of six photographs show the wonderful under-valued scenery that was part of the short branch line from Connell Ferry to Ballachullish which was closed to goods in 1965 and to passengers in March of 1966.

Ex LMSR IVATT Class 2 2-6-0 #46460 steams alongside the shores of Loch Linnhe north of Benderloch with a Ballachullish to Oban train in June 1962.

Roy M. Crombie

Ex LMSR IVATT Class 2 2-6-0 #46460 skirts the east shore of Loch Linnhe at Cuill Bay with a two coach afternoon service from Ballachullish to Oban in June 1962.

Roy M. Crombie

B.R. STD Class 2 2-6-0 #78052 steams south of Duror alongside Loch Linnhe with a Ballachullish to Connell Ferry mixed goods, train in June 1962. The authors Triumph Herald saloon car nicely dates this composition as it is parked on the side of the A828.

Roy M. Crombie

Unidentified **B.R.C.W. Class 27 Bo-Bo diesel electric** rattles an Oban to Ballachullish train alongside the shores of Loch Linnhe in February 1966.

courtesy G.N.S.R.A. Collection

B.R.C.W. Class 27 Bo-Bo diesel electric #D5347 heads a reasonably mixed Ballachullish to Connell Ferry goods south of Duror in May 1963. Noticeable in the consist are several vacuum fitted presflo alumina wagons returning empty from Ballachullish yard where they were unloaded for the British Aluminium Co's works at nearby Kinlochleven. This traffic came from Burntisland in Fife.

Ken Nuttall

B.R.C.W. Class 27 Bo-Bo diesel electric #D5356 heads a northbound passenger train from Oban to Ballachullish along the shore of Loch Linnhe in May 1963, with the mountains of Morven noticeable on the west side of the loch.

Ken Nuttall

B.R. STD 4MT 2-6-4 TANK #80092 heads a featherweight Callander to Killin goods train north of the delightful Perthshire village of Strathyre in September 1964.

Roy M. Crombie

Ex LNER B.I. 4-6-0 #61263 approaches Silverhillock with the daily Dundee to Kingsmuir and return trip working in May 1996, on the rump of the former line to Forfar.

John Spencer Gilks

A 2-Car METRO-CAMMELL Class 101 D.M.U. approaches Tayport with a service from Dundee seen on the north bank of the River Tay estuary in April 1965.

Roy M. Crombie

E.E. Class 40. I Co-Co I diesel electric #40.192 splutters away from the D.C.L. distillery at Burghead with an afternoon rake of empty 35-ton BRT vacuum fitted bulk grain wagons, now shorn of their former whisky brand logos bound for Doncaster in May 1978.

Geo. C. O'Hara

Unidentified **Ex LNER B1 4-6-0** approaches Largo with a Thornton Junction to Anstruther train on the Fife Coast line in July 1965.

Roy M. Crombie

E.E. Class 08 0-6-0 diesel shunter #08.515 hauls a mixed lightweight trip freight comprising a pair of private owner 4-wheel air braked wagons and a brake van from Auchmutty Mill near Markinch to Thornton Yard during July 1986. This traffic was symptomatic of the residual low density freight volumes carried by the B.R. Speedlink Service on the remaining Scottish branch lines.

Geo. C. O'Hara

Unidentified **E.E. Class 40 I Co-Co I diesel electric** approaches Bogside with a Stirling to Edinburgh service via Alloa and the Forth Bridge in April 1968, shortly before withdrawal of the passenger service on this route.

Roy M. Crombie

E.E. Class 20 Bo-Bo diesel electric #20.111 shunts several United Molasses vacuum fitted mollasses tank wagons at the Menstrie D.C.L. plant in April 1978. In pristine condition, these wagons in their claret and blue livery with UM logo were among the most attractive on British Railways.

Geo. C. O'Hara

B.R.C.W. Class 26 Bo-Bo diesel electric #26.023 hauls a single high capacity Polybulk grain wagon down the truncated Leven Branch with a trip freight working from Thornton Yard to the D.C.L. distillery at Cameron Bridge in February 1989.

Geo. G. O'Hara

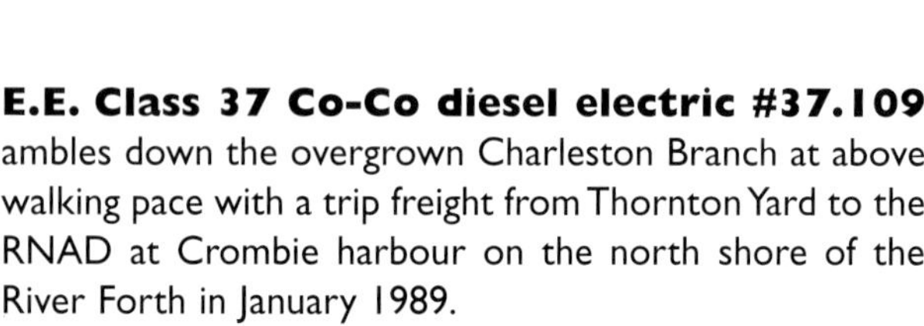

E.E. Class 37 Co-Co diesel electric #37.109 ambles down the overgrown Charleston Branch at above walking pace with a trip freight from Thornton Yard to the RNAD at Crombie harbour on the north shore of the River Forth in January 1989.

Geo. G. O'Hara

Ex LNER J37 0-6-0 #64633 passes Twechar on the Kilsyth branch with a lengthy coal train for Cadder Yard from Queenzieburn Colliery in March 1963.

Douglas Hume

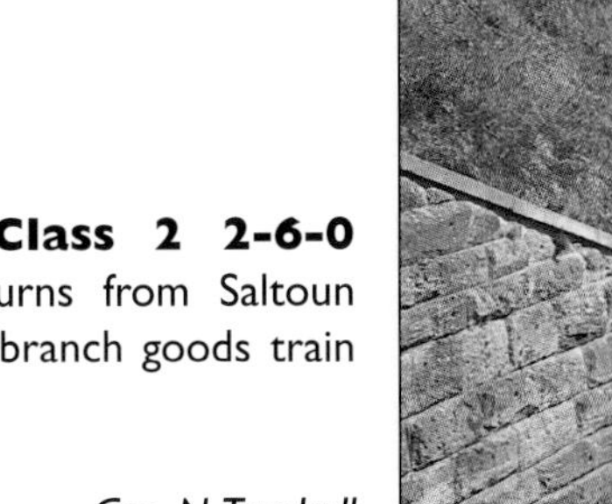

Ex LMSR Class 2 2-6-0 #46462 returns from Saltoun with the daily branch goods train in April 1964.

Geo. N. Turnbull

B.R. SULZER Class 25 Bo-Bo diesel electric #D7607 resplendent in original weathered two-tone green livery waits at the then terminus of the Penicuik Branch with a return trip working to Millerhill Yard in March 1967, shortly before closure of the branch.

Geo. N. Turnbull

Unidentified **E.C. Class 08 0-6-0 diesel shunter** hauls a short trip freight on the rust covered rails of the little used Balerno Branch in July 1967.

D. E. D. Blades

Ex LMSR CRAB 2-6-0 #42805 approaches Brackenhill Junction with a trip freight from the short Catrine Branch bound for Ayr Falkland yard in June 1963.

Derek Cross (courtesy David M. Cross)

Ex CALEY 3F 0-6-0 #57604 climbs away from Inches Junction towards Glespin with a loaded coal train from nearby Kennox Colliery on the short Carmacoup spur, bound for Mossend yard on the Muirkirk to Lanark Branch in June 1962.

Derek Cross (courtesy David M. Cross)

B.R. STD Class 3 2-6-0 #77017 east of Sandilands near the course of the infant River Clyde with a Muirkirk to Lanark service in April 1962.

Roy M. Crombie

E.E. Class 20 Bo-Bo diesel electrics #'s 20.203 & 20.028 amble uphill beyond Drongan with a rake of Ayrshire coal in HAA wagons bound for Killoch Washery from Ayr Falkland yard in February 1987.

Geo. C. O'Hara

B.R.C.W. Class 26 Bo-Bo diesel electric #'s 26.002 & 26.001 approach Bank Junction on the re-instated branch to Knockshinnoch with a lengthy rake of coal in air braked HAA wagons bound for Killoch Washery via Ayr Falkland yard in September 1989.

Geo. C. O'Hara

Ex LMSR (CALEY) 3F 0-6-0 #57627 comes off the Snodgrass (Bogside) Branch with a rake of vacuum fitted loaded gunpowder vans comprising a trip working from the ICI explosives works at Ardeer to Ayr Falkland Yard in July 1963. This working ran wrong line for about half a mile until the correct line was traversed at the nearby Bogside signal box.

W. A. C. Smith

Ex LMSR (CALEY) 3F's 0-6-0 #'s 57644 & 57618 (The Twins) ease a loaded coal train from either Littlemill or Whitehill Colliery to Ayr Harbour near Belston Junction in August 1960.

Colour Rail #Sc722 - John Agnew collection

Unidentified **EX LMSR 4MT 2-6-4T** approaches Bogston between Greenock and Port Glasgow with the Clyde estuary visible beyond, whilst heading a train from Wemyss Bay to Glasgow Central in April 1965.

Roy M. Crombie

DUTCH LIVERIED B.R.C.W. Class 26 Bo-Bo diesel electric #26.038 shunts a short rake of air braked TTA caustic soda liquor wagons from Ayr Falkland Yard into the I.C.I. Ardeer Misk Siding Branch in December 1987.

Geo. C. O'Hara

E.E. Class 37 Co-Co diesel electric #37.018 threads the Lyndeoch suburb of Greenock with the cranes of the then moribund Scott Lithgow Cartsburn and Cartsdyke shipyards visible beyond. The train is the weekly Saturday Coatbridge Containerbase to Greenock Ocean Terminal service then run for the German Shipping Line Hapag-Lloyd and is seen in the summer of 1986.

Geo. C. O'Hara

E.E. Class 37 Co-Co diesel electric #37.170 ambles down the short Dalmuir Branch with the cranes of the former John Brown Clydebank shipyard (then operating as U.I.E.) noticeable beyond. The train is the daily trip working from Mossend yard to the Chivas Bros bottling plant conveying bulk malt whisky in ISO containers from the Chivas plant at Keith, and is seen in February 1988.

Geo. C. O'Hara

Section 3

SELECTION OF SCOTTISH LOCOMOTIVE SHEDS AND DEPOTS

This section of the book depicts only 16 out of an active total of 83 locomotive sheds, depots, sub sheds and stabling points which existed around the time of the British Railways Scottish Region zenith of operation in the late 1950's. As the section title implies the emphasis on this part of the book is to show as much of the loco shed real estate and functionality as possible with secondary emphasis on any type of traction stabled in the photographic assemblage.

GLASGOW EASTFIELD #65A Depicted in April 1978 with an extensive laid over stud of blue liveried diesel locomotives then active in the haulage of passenger and freight trains throughout the Scottish region.

Geo. C. O'Hara

Part of the coaling stage at **GLASGOW BALORNOCK #65B** seen to good effect in November 1963 with 2 ex LMSR Class 5 4-6-0's #45194 & 45417 seen alongside ex LNER A3 4-6-2 #60094 Colorado.

Colour Rail #Sc 1020I
Geo. M. Staddon

A more general view of **GLASGOW BALORNOCK #65B** in June 1963 showing several steam locomotives on shed and a portion of the once ubiquitous post war built Glasgow Corporation tenement housing stock in the background.

Alan Carlaw

Top left:
GLASGOW POLMADIE #66A seen in July 1968 and showing EE CL20 Bo-Bo, EE CL37 Co-Co, and Clayton CL17 Bo-Bo diesel electric locomotives outside the shed.
Dougald Cameron

Top right:
MOTHERWELL #66B seen in February 1963 with a predominance of ex LMSR (CALEY) 0-6-0 tender locomotives on show. Note the spent ash lying adjacent to the tracks.
Ronnie Provan

Left: top:
COATBRIDGE KIPPS #65E is passed by a recently introduced CL303 E.M.U. in October 1961 resplendent in mock Caledonian Railway blue livery. The scene depicts the transition period from steam to diesel traction when several N.B.L. built diesel hydraulic and B.R. built diesel mechanical shunters are on view.
Roy M. Crombie

Left middle:
OBAN #63C seen in July 1962 at the height of the transition from steam to diesel traction. Noticeable in this view are the depot turntable, coaling tower, diesel oil tank wagons, coal wagons and a few locos beyond.
Alan Carlaw

Left bottom:
GREENOCK LADYBURN #66D is seen on a cold misty January 1966 during its last year of operation where the small amount of traction on show indicates closure of the depot is not far away.
Roy M. Crombie

POLMONT #65K seen in March 1964 with a reasonable stud of locomotives including ex LNER J37 0-6-0's #'s 64537 & 64636 in steam.

Robin Nelson

MUIRKIRK #67B (a sub shed of HURLFORD) seen in May 1962 with B.R. standard Class 3 2-6-0 #77018 on display in near ex-works condition.

Douglas Hume

DUMFRIES #68B, the six road former GSWR brick built shed is seen in April 1961 with ex LMSR, Caley and B.R. standard locos in steam and on show. Note the sheer legs structure at the right side of the depot used for lifting locomotives to change wheels and motion.

Roy M. Crombie

MONTROSE #62B (a sub shed of DUNDEE) seen in June 1963 with ex LNER J37 0-6-0 #64620 about to be coaled from the manually operated loco coaling facility.

Douglas Paul

FORT WILLIAM #63B seen in the smoke shrouded distance as B.R. STD Class 5. 4-6-0 #73105 in charge of a Mallaig-Glasgow train heads south. At this time in June 1960 the main West Highland shed housed several active steam locomotives.

Roy M. Crombie

The small two-road **SUB SHED OF ALLOA** is seen in June 1965 as an unidentified Ex LNER J38 0-6-0 chugs past this still active sub shed of **DUNFERMLINE #62C** with a coal train from neighbouring Alloa yard bound for nearby Kincardine power station. The siding on the right served the Skol brewery and conveyed malt in BR grain wagons up until the 1980's.

David C. Smith

THORNTON #62A SHED seen in April 1966 where ex LNER and ex W.D. locos are seen in attendance. The structure on the right was one of the winding flowers for the former Rothes Colliery complex closed by serious flooding shortly after its opening by the N.C.B. in the 1950's.

David C. Smith

EDINBURGH ST. MARGARETS #64A SHED seen in the period immediately after the end of steam traction with B.R. CL24 Bo-Bo, BR. CL47 Co-Co and Clayton CL17 Bo-Bo diesel electrics all resplendent in their fast becoming grimy two-tone green livery schemes with half height yellow warning panels.

Geo. N. Turnbull

Section 4

SELECTION OF SCOTTISH MAIN LINE, BRANCH AND SUBURBAN STATIONS

This section of the book shows only a fraction of the several hundred mainly unique stations that were extant under the operation of the former British Railways Scottish Region. Considering that most of these stations were categorised as "suburban, or rural wayside halts, this book has attempted to illustrate a reasonable spectrum of station types with various train formations included in the respective picture. Several of the stations depicted are station in name only having lost their passenger status prior to the time of being photographed. Remarkable throughout the following scenes is the lack of vandalism to these structures reflecting a time when property was revered and not seen as a source of destructive amusement.

Unidentified **Ex LMSR Class 5 4-6-0 SWINDON Class 120 D.M.U. and CLAYTON Class 17 Bo-Bo diesel electric** make an impressive composition with westbound trains at the former cavernous Edinburgh Princes Street station in September 1965.

Geo. N. Turnbull

Ex LMSR DUCHESS Class 4-6-2 #46249 "CITY OF SHEFFIELD" is seen at the head of a southbound express in Glasgow St. Enoch station in a hazy day during July 1962.

Dougald Cameron

Ex LMSR DUCHESS Class 4-6-2 #46256 "SIR WILLIAM A. STAINER F.R.S." makes an awe inspiring sight as it is photographed at the head of a London bound overnight "football special" train in Glasgow Central Station in April 1964.

Dougald Cameron

Above:
BR STD Class 5 4-6-0 #73150 gets ready to leave Glasgow Buchanan Street station with a train for Dundee in September 1966.

Alan Carlaw

Below:
Ex LMSR FAIRBURN 4MT 2-6-4T #42127 stops at Clydebank Riverside station adjacent to the world famous John Brown shipyard with a Dalmuir Riverside to Rutherglen train in July 1962.

W.A. C. Smith

Above:
Unidentified **Ex LNER B.1. 4-6-0** leaves Glasgow Buchanan Street station with a train for Perth in October 1966.

Robin Nelson

Below left:
Ex LMSR FAIRBURN 4MT #42197 leaves Partick West station with a Possil to Rutherglen train via Glasgow Central Low level in April 1964, passing a recently marshalled cattle train from nearby Merklands Lairage.

Roy M. Crombie

Below:
METRO-CAMMELL Class 101 3-Car D.M.U. splutters away from Kirkintilloch station with a train for Glasgow Queen Street in August 1964.

Roy M. Crombie

B.R. STD 4MT 2-6-4T #80077 stops at the rural wayside station of Newmilns in the Irvine valley with a service from Darvel to Kilmarnock in April 1964.

Roy Hamilton

PARK ROYAL BUILT 4-WHEEL RAILBUS #Sc79971 frames the south gable of Dalmellington station in the Doon valley as it waits between rosters on the Ayr and Kilmarnock railbus service in October 1963.

Geo N. Turnbull

With the closure only days away the tall signalbox and under used station at Muirkirk host a **GLOUCESTER 2-Car Class 100 D.M.U.** recently arrived on a service from Lanark in October 1964.

courtesy G.N.S.R.A. Collection

B.R. STD 4MT 2-6-4T #80023 waits at Kirkcudbright station with a two coach working to Dumfries in March 1963.

Derek Cross
(courtesy David M. Cross)

Ex LNER A3 4-6-2 #60052 "PRINCE PALATINE" takes on water and prepares to leave Hawick station with a northbound goods train in December 1965.

Douglas Paul

A GLOUCESTER 2-Car Class 100 D.M.U. decants a smattering of passengers attired in the style of the era from a Galashiels to Edinburgh via Peebles service at Innerleithen Station in January 1962.

Geo. N. Turnbull

Callander station viewed from the footbridge with Ben Ledi partly visible beyond sees **Ex LMSR FAIRBURN 4MT 2-6-4T #42468** letting off steam prior to working a service to Stirling in June 1963.

Roy M. Crombie

Callander station viewed from the platform in June 1964 sees an unusual visitor in the form of **Ex LNER V2 2-6-2 #60818** waiting to depart with a service to Edinburgh in June 1964.

Robin Nelson

Ex LNER J37 0-6-0 #64580 runs round the infrequent goods train service from Cadder Yard at Aberfoyle in July 1958. The timber station buildings look far from dilapidated despite this location losing its passenger services some seven years earlier.

Colour Rail #Sc508/W. Oliver

Ex LNER B.I. 4-6-0 #61244 "STRANG STEEL" heads a Comrie to Crieff and Gleneagles service at the ornate Crieff station in June 1963.

Geo. N. Turnbull

Ex LMSR REBUILT ROYAL SCOT 4-6-0 #46166 "LONDON RIFLE BRIGADE" prepares to leave the south end of Perth station with a southbound fish train comprised mainly of vacuum fitted blue spot insul fish vans in April 1964. Note the handful of train spotters on the platform.

Douglas Paul

Ex LMSR Class 5 4-6-0 #44715 blasts out of the north end of Perth station with an express from Glasgow Buchanan Street to Aberdeen via the Strathmore route in April 1965.

John Spencer Gilks

Ex LMSR IVATT Class 4 2-6-0 #43137 chuffs away from Rumbling Bridge station with a Perth to Glasgow Buchanan Street service via the Devon Valley Line in April 1960.

Roy M. Crombie

METRO CAMMELL 2-Car Class 101 D.M.U. pauses at Rumbling Bridge station with an afternoon Stirling to Perth service via the Devon Valley Line in May 1964.

Douglas Hume

Unidentified **B.R.C.W. Class 27 Bo-Bo diesel electric** re-starts a Glasgow Buchanan Street to Oban via Callandar service from Loch Awe station in September 1965.

Roy Hamilton

B.R.C.W. Class 27 Bo-Bo diesel electric #D5367 brings an afternoon train from Oban into the terminus of Ballachullish station in March 1963.

Ken Nuttall

Ex LNER J38. 0-6-0. #65914 in charge of an east-bound coal train passes a **METRO-CAMMELL Class 101 3-car D.M.U.** At Burntisland station in July 1966 where some of the cranes from the then busy shipyard are seen in the distance.

David C. Smith

Ex LNER BI. 4-6-0 #61340 shunts the station at St. Andrews in June 1965 as a **METRO-CAMMELL Class 101 3-car D.M.U.** approaches with a service from Dundee.

Douglas Paul

Ex LNER B.I. 4-6-0 #61293 plays second fiddle to a cornucopia of 1960's vintage cars and vans in the station car park at Wormit, as it trundles past with a trip freight from Dundee to Tayport in April 1965.

Roy M. Crombie

Ex LNER A4. 4-6-2 #60016 "SILVER KING" at Dundee West station with an express service to Glasgow Buchanan Street in December 1964.

Hugh Morton

Unidentified **B.R.C.W. Class 26 Bo-Bo diesel electric** in charge of an afternoon Aberfeldy to Ballinluig Junction service halts at Grandtully Station in March 1965. The ex LNER Thomson designed brake coach now reposes at the S.R.P.S. site at Bo'ness.

Geo. N. Turnbull

A pair of **E.E. Class 20 Bo-Bo diesel electrics #'s D8104 & D8072** leave Fort William with an evening train for Glasgow Queen Street in July 1962.

Colour Rail #DE1603/C. Woodhead

Mallaig Station seen in the pouring rain synonymous with this West of Scotland location as **B.R.C.W. Class 27 Bo-Bo diesel electric #D5358** leaves the then busy branch line terminus with a train for Glasgow Queen Street in June 1962.

Roy M. Crombie

N.B.L. Class 21 Bo-Bo diesel electric #D6150 trundles through the wayside station of Knock with its adjacent whisky distillery and rail connected private siding whilst working the Speyside goods service in June 1965.

Roy M. Crombie

Ex LMSR Class 5 4-6-0 #45461 shunts the goods only station at Kirriemuir, which still possessed an impressive and well built station building, whilst in charge of a trip working from nearby Forfar in June 1963.

Douglas Paul

Ex LNER J37 0-6-0 #64587 shunts the goods only station at Brechin with a trip freight working from Montrose under a magnificently colourful afternoon sky in November 1963.

Douglas Paul

A CRAVENS Class 105 2-Car D.M.U. stops at Dinnet Station with a Deeside line service between Aberdeen and Ballater in Februrary 1966, shortly before closure of this line.

Courtesy G.N.S.R.A. Collection

Unidentified **N.B.L. Class 21 Bo-Bo diesel electric** halts at the impressive timber built Keith Town station whilst working an Aberdeen to Elgin via Rothes service in June 1965.

Roy M. Crombie

Unidentified **N.B.L. Class 21 Bo-Bo diesel electric** at Peterhead Station at the head of a two-coach train for Maud Junction in April 1965.

David C. Smith

B.R. STD 4MT 2-6-4T #80115 ambles into Strichen station with a relief Aberdeen to Fraserburgh featherweight parcels train in June 1960.

Roy Hamilton

A busy scene at Fraserburgh Station in September 1963 with unidentified **N.B.L. Class 21 Bo-Bo diesel electrics** on fish empties and passenger trains from and to Aberdeen, as well as a **CRAVENS Class 105 2-car D.M.U.** on a service to St. Combs.

Courtesy G.N.S.R.A. Collection

B.R. STD Class 2. 2-6-0 #76104 leaking steam and with a young interloper on the foot-plate, poses at Banff Station with an afternoon service to Tillynaught Junction in June 1964.

Courtesy G.N.S.R.A. Collection

Unidentified **N.B.L. Class 21 Bo-Bo diesel electric** waits at the former G.N.S.R. Station at Lossiemouth with an afternoon train for Elgin in March 1963.

Courtesy G.N.S.R.A. Collection

B.R. SULZER Class 24 Bo-Bo diesel electric #D5114 approaches Scotscalder with a lengthy Inverness to the Far North line mixed freight train in June 1966.

Roy M. Crombie

Unidentified **B.R.C.W. Class 26 Bo-Bo diesel electric** at Wick station with a short train for Georgmas Junction (and Inverness) in June 1966. Note the blue spot insul fish vans in the bay platform and the period motor vehicles.

Roy M. Crombie

An unidentified pair of **B.R.C.W. Class 26 Bo-Bo diesel electrics** repose at Thurso station in April 1982, when this line still had a variety of freight traffic and loco hauled passenger trains.

John Spencer Gilks

Section 5

SELECTION OF SCOTTISH GOODS AND MARSHALLING YARDS

This section of the book combines two quite distinctive areas of railway operation within the one heading solely because of the term "yard". Goods yards were either the point of despatch or delivery of the commodity carried by rail, whereas marshalling yards were intermediate facilities where either wagon to train or vice versa aspects of train formation occurred, but invariably neither despatch nor delivery took place. Goods yards outnumbered marshalling yards in Scotland by a factor of nearly 100:1. Consequently representation of the yards represented in this section reflects this imbalance.

Unidentified **N.B.L. 0-4-0 diesel hydraulic shunter** is seen amidst the vastness of Leith Citadel goods yard in July 1964.

David C. Smith

Ex LNER J36 0-6-0 #65282 is seen shunting the once extensive upper marshalling yard at Bathgate during June 1963 when most of the traffic emanated from the then bustling West Lothian coalfield .

W.A. C. Smith

B.R. STD Class 2 2-6-0 #78050 prepares to leave the extensive and busy goods yard at Chapelhall, Lanarkshire with a trip freight for nearby Mossend yard in March 1962.

Douglas Hume

A GLOUCESTER Class 100 2-Car D.M.U. passes the soon to be abandoned goods yard at Peebles whilst working a service from Galashiels to Edinburgh in February 1962.

Roy M. Crombie

Ex LNER J38 0-6-0 #65914 shunts the traditional Scottish coal 'ree' in Gullane goods yard with a trip working from Millerhill yard in June 1964.

Geo. N. Turnbull

CLAYTON Class 17 Bo-Bo diesel electric #D8583 recently re-painted in drab B.R. rail blue livery shunts the spacious goods yard at Haddington on the short branch from Longniddry Junction in September 1967.

Geo. N. Turnbull

BR Class 08 0-6-0 diesel mechanical shunter #D3730 makes a fine period pose in the coal yard at the former Currie Station on the Balerno branch during October 1967, whilst shunting several rust encrusted 16-ton mineral wagons.

Geo. N. Turnbull

Ex LNER B1 4-6-0 #61134 shunts the traditional goods yard at Catrine, Ayrshire with the then regular trip working from Ayr Falkland yard during the spring of 1964.

Roy Hamilton

E.E. Class 20 Bo-Bo diesel electric #20.111 brings an empty ex LMS unfitted bulk grain wagon and brake van from the nearby Skol brewery into Alloa marshalling yard in April 1978.

Geo. C. O'Hara

Ex LNER J38 0-6-0 #65912 shunts the yard at Tillicoultry, Clackmannanshire whilst working a trip freight service on the then truncated Devon Valley Line in June 1965.

David C. Smith

Former **W.D. 2-8-0 #90386** leaves the extensive marshalling yard at Townhill, Fife, with a westbound loaded coal train made up with different grades of domestic coal from several local collieries bound for Alloa yard in May 1964.

W. A. C. Smith

Unidentified **EE Class 20 Bo-Bo diesel electric** shunts the dilapidated goods yard at Milnathort, Kinross with one of the last trip workings on the former Perth-Edinburgh via Glenfarg main line in a bleak and dull December afternoon in 1969.

D. E. D. Blades

CRAVENS Class 105 2-Car D.M.U. stops at Newport-on-Tay East where the traditional goods yard with covered coal depot is seen to good effect whilst working a St. Andrews to Arbroath service in July 1966.

Roy M. Crombie

A Panoramic view of Dundee West goods yard showing part of the Tay estuary, the famous railway bridge, in addition to packed railway facilities in June 1964.

Hugh Morton

Unidentified **B.R.C.W. Class 26 Bo-Bo diesel electric** shunts the soon to be closed goods yard at Maryfield, Dundee on the truncated Lochee branch in August 1967.

D. E. D. Blades

Ex L.N.E.R. B.I. 4-6-0 #61246 prepares to leave the Perthshire goods yard at Bankfoot with a short freight for Perth yard between snow showers in January 1962.

Colour Rail #Sc157/N. Forrest

Below:

B.R. STD Class 5 4-6-0 #73008 shunts the still extant goods yard at Justinhaugh, Angus with a Forfar to Careston trip freight in May 1964.

John Spencer Gilks

Below:

EX L.M.S.R. Class 2P 4-4-0 #40603 passes through the throat of the then extensive goods yard at Peterhead whilst working a through train to Aberdeen in June 1955.

Colour Rail #Sc980/J. F. Henton

Below:

The extensive and busy yard and sidings at Fraserburgh in September 1963. Whilst express fish traffic in XP (express passenger) 12-ton blue spot insul vans was the staple traffic, this branch also conveyed coal, general goods and laterly North Sea pipe line traffic before closure in 1979.

Douglas Hume

ANDREW BARCLAY Class 06 0-4-0 diesel mechanical shunter #D2423 shunts the still function goods yard at Oldmeldrum where agricultural produce is the staple traffic in the autumn of 1965.

Colour Rail #DE833/T. J. Edgington

Unidentified **B.R. SULZER Class 24 Bo-Bo diesel electric** shunts the derelict goods yard at Banff in April 1968, shortly before total closure of the line from Tillynaught Junction.

Keith G. Jones/G.N.S.R.A. Collection

Unidentified **B.R.C.W. Class 26 Bo-Bo diesel electric** shunts the north pier goods yard at Kyle of Lochalsh with a rake of four wheel traditional goods wagons in September 1962, shortly after total dieselisation of the line.

Roy M. Crombie

B.R. STD Class 2 2-6-0 #78052 shunts the small but busy goods yard at Ballachullish in June 1962, where bulk alumina in vacuum fitted presflo wagons for the nearby aluminium works at Kinlochleven was the staple freight traffic, in addition to coal and general goods.

Roy M. Crombie

Oban goods yard seen in July 1962 with an unidentified **B.R.C.W. Class 27 Bo-Bo diesel electric** seen in the distance among several rakes of goods wagons. The steam shed and its active coaling facilities can be seen on the left.

Alan Carlaw

Unidentified **Ex L.M.S.R. Class 5 4-6-0** shunts the extensive goods yard at Crieff with the daily trip freight working from Perth yard in February 1964.

Roy M. Crombie

E.E. Class 37 Co-Co diesel electrics #'s 37.049/037/040 triple head a B.S.C. Hunterston to B.S.C. Ravenscraig air braked iron-ore block train away from Mossend marshalling yard in June 1989. Railway contraction in Scotland in the 1990's has resulted in this yard now being the hub for railfreight operations in Scotland.

Tom. H. Noble

E.E. Class 37 0-6-0 #37.147 leaves Cadder North marshalling yard with the afternoon mixed goods train to Fort William in November 1978. Notable in the train consist are several vacuum fitted covhop wagons conveying aluminia from Invergordon.

Tom. H. Noble

E.E. Class 37 Co-Co diesel electric #37.027 resplendent in large yellow ends shunts several 16-ton MCV vacuum fitted coal wagons at the extensive Pinkston goods and mineral depot in August 1981. This scene was once redolent of many goods depots throughout Scotland when coal was the dominant domestic fuel. Of interest is the use of empty oil drums used to form parietals to retain stocks of coal. The white kegs in the foreground are used for the transport of beer.

Tom. H. Noble

Part of the extensive traditional ex-Caledonian Railway goods and mineral depot at Maryhill Central is seen to reasonable effect to the right of **Ex-L.M.S.R. 4MT 2-6-4T #42200** shunting a rake of empty suburban passenger stock at this former Glasgow location in October 1962.

Roy M. Crombie

B.R. STD Class 2 2-6-0 #78026 prepares to leave the former goods yard at the junction station of Wigtown with the Isle of Whithorn branch freight train in July 1964, the last year of operation of this line.

Courtesy G.N.S.R.A. Collection

Section 6

SELECTION OF SCOTTISH RAILWAY OVER BRIDGES AND VIADUCTS

This section of the book attempts to depict several of the thousands of bridges, viaducts and accesses that formed an integrated element of the former British Railways Scottish Region route mileage. A few of these structures became famous Scottish and international landmarks, however many befell the action of demolition crews when their routes were closed and lifted. Others remain as relics to a bygone era, whilst the seemingly ever contracting list of those remaining on the asset list become encumbered with the inordinate cost of "creative accounting" which somehow construes to belie their functionality.

Ex LMSR FAIRBURN 4MT 2-6-4T #42127 crosses the River Kelvin Bridge after leaving Partick Central (Kelvin Hall) station with a Possil to Rutherglen working in September 1964.

Douglas Hume

An unidentified **E.E. Class 08 0-6-0 diesel mechanical shunter** trundles a trip freight working from Partick Central to Yoker Yard over a ubiquitous design of rivetted plate girder bridge in the Glasgow suburb of Whiteinch in April 1978.

Geo. C. O'Hara

Ex L.M.S.R. FAIRBURN 4MT 2-6-4T #42195 crosses a common design of lattice web rivetted girder bridge in Clydebank with a Dalmuir to Rutherglen passenger train in July 1962. Note the Glasgow Corporation Cunarder tram #132 on Dumbarton Road, sparse road traffic and a spread of bill board designs redolent of that decade.

W.A. C. Smith

Ex L.M.S.R. FAIRBURN 4MT 2-6-4T #42197 crosses the stone arch and plate girder River Kelvin viaduct west of Maryhill Central station in Glasgow with a Clydebank to Possil workman's train in October 1962.

Roy M. Crombie

A Hybrid 4-Car D.M.U. consisting of **METRO-CAMMELL Class 101 & B.R. DERBY Class 107 units** makes a smokey departure from Strathaven over the Caledonian Railway designed plate girder built viaduct north of Strathaven Central station with a train for Glasgow Central in May 1963. The other viaduct carried the then closed route to Hamilton via Quarter.

Roy M. Crombie

Below:
EX H.R. 4-6-0 #104 crosses the brick built Devol viaduct in Upper Port Glasgow with a special railtour working from Greenock Princes Pier in the spring of 1965. Noticeable in this view are the recently constructed Firth of Clyde dry dock with a barely visible Blue Funnel Line vessel under repair and the giant level luffing dockside cranes, which were designed and built in Glasgow.

Roy M. Crombie

Above:
E.E. Class 37 Co-Co diesel electric #37.097 trundles over the tiny brick and steel over-bridge over the B706 road in the hamlet of Barrmill with a Mossend yard to Giffen R.N.A.D. trip freight in November 1987.

Geo. C. O'Hara

Recently re-painted in B.R. rail blue **E.E. Class 20 Bo-Bo diesel electric #D8104** trundles a rake of Ayr Harbour to Littlemill colliery 16-ton mineral wagon empties over Rankinston east masonry viaduct in November 1971.

Derek Cross (Courtesy David M. Cross)

The last passenger train from Ayr to Dalmellington crosses the impressive multi-arch masonry viaduct at Dalrymple hauled by **B.R. ST Class 3 2-6-0 #77016** in April 1964. This structure continues to be used by heavy trains conveying coal from the extant open-cast mines in the upper Doon valley.

Derek Cross (Courtesy of David M. Cross)

B.R. STD Class 4 2-6-0 #76093 rattles across the multi-arch bowstring girder viaduct at the south end of Loch Ken with a Stranraer to Dumfries goods train in September 1964.

Roy M. Crombie

B.R. STD 4MT 2-6-4T #80061 is dwarfed by the mass of the Big Water of Fleet brick and stone built viaduct with a light-weight Stranraer to Dumfries working in September 1964.

Roy M. Crombie

A GLOUCESTER Class 100 2-Car D.M.U. crosses the rivetted Caledonian Railway designed fish belly plate girder multi-span bridge over the River Tweed at Cardrona with an Edinburgh Waverley to Galashiels via Peebles service in September 1961.

Roy M. Crombie

Bottom:
Ex L.N.E.R. V2 2-6-2 #60813 crosses Shankend viaduct with a southbound Waverley Route mixed freight in June 1964.

Colour Rail #Sc600/J. B. Snell

Unidentified **Ex L.N.E.R. V2. 2-6-2** crosses Slitrig viaduct whilst heading a lengthy Carlisle Kingmoor to Millerhill yard Waverley Route mixed freight conveying several empty insul fish vans in the summer of 1963. Also in the consist are several new motor cars being conveyed by train before the establishment of the U.K. motorway network.

Gordon Hall - courtesy Geo. N. Turnbull

Ex L.M.S.R. Class 2 2-6-2T #40151 crosses the multi arch rivetted bowstring girder Sandilands viaduct over the infant River Clyde with a Muirkirk to Lanark train in August 1959.

Roy M. Crombie

Ex L.M.S.R Class 5 4-6-0 #44953 crosses the A70 plate girder overbridge east of Inches Station with an afternoon Muirkirk to Lanark train in April 1962. Branching off from the left can be seen the short Carmacoup spur up towards Kennox colliery, which provided the last eastbound regular freight traffic on this line which closed entirely in October 1964.

Roy M. Crombie

A pair of unidentified **E.E. Class 08 0-6-0 diesel mechanical shunters** trundle on intermediate trip freight working over the impressive multi-arch plate girder Ross viaduct near Motherwell in June 1960.

W. A. C. Smith

Ex L.M.S.R. Class 2 2-6-0 #46468 comes off the impressive multi-span Alloa viaduct with an Alloa to Grangemouth goods working in March 1964. Noticeable beyond the train is the control tower which worked the mechanical turning section of the bridge which was swivelled to allow the passage of small vessels up the River Forth to Alloa harbour. The short spur to the left served the RNAD stores complex at Bandeath and became the terminus for this line following the closure of the bridge in 1969.

Roy M. Crombie

E.E. Class 20 Bo-Bo #20.111 is about to approach the traditional plate girder bridge over the River Devon on the short Menstrie branch with an afternoon trip freight to Grangemouth yard comprising empty United Molasses air braked tank wagons in April 1978.

Geo. C. O'Hara

Ex L.M.S.R. IVATT Class 4 2-6-0 #43136 crosses the stone and steel girder River Devon viaduct east of Dollar with a Glasgow Buchanan Street to Perth train via the Devon Valley Line in April 1960.

Roy M. Crombie

Ex L.N.E.R. J37 0-6-0 #64606 works a trip comprising a variety of empty 21-ton hopper wagons over the multi-arch masonry Leslie viaduct en route from Leslie to Thornton yard in August 1965.

Colour Rail #Sc964/Ron White

Ex L.N.E.R. A3 4-6-2 #60052 "PRINCE PALATINE" resplendent in sleek German style smoke deflectors blasts up the multi arch brick-built approach viaduct to the River Tay bridge with a southbound Dundee Perth & London Shipping Company Charter freight working in November 1965.

Hugh Morton

Unidentified **Ex CALEY MACINTOSH 0-4-4T** ambles over the double lattice girder bridge over the River Tay at Logierait with an afternoon mixed train from Aberfeldy to Ballinluig Junction in July 1961. This bridge was not dismantled following closure of the line in 1965.

John Spencer Gilks

E.E. Class 37 Co-Co #37.422 crosses the North British Railway designed typical West Highland hybrid lattice and plate girder viaduct south of Rannoch Moor with a Blyth to Mallaig Junction train comprised of vacuum fitted alumina hopper wagons in May 1987.

Tom. H. Noble

Ex L.N.E.R. K1. 2-6-0 #62052 crosses the famous mass arched reinforced concrete viaduct at Glenfinnan with a rake of empty fish vans at the head of a train for Mallaig in July 1959.

Colour Rail #Sc437/J. G. Wallace

B.R. STD Class 2 2-6-0 #78052 crosses the twin span rivetted truss type girder bridge at Creagan Narrows with an Oban to Ballachullish train in June 1962. Remaining in situ for three decades after closure of the railway, this bridge was recently dismantled and replaced with a new road bridge carrying the A828 Connel Ferry to Ballachullish road.

Roy M. Crombie

B.R. STD Class 2 2-6-0 #78052 leaves the impressive Connell Ferry cantilever bridge with a Ballachullish to Oban train in May 1962. Following closure of the railway in 1966 this bridge was converted for total road usage and is now an integral part of the A828.

Roy M. Crombie

Section 7

SELECTION OF SCOTTISH INDUSTRIAL AND PRIVATE RAILWAY SIDINGS

This section of the book depicts a small number of sidings, branches and yards from a once impressive total of several hundred which were the former life blood of the Scottish railway system, existing in nearly every town, city or industrial establishment throughout the country. The issue of respective asset ownership is collectively dismissed as is that of some of the wagons and locomotives shown in the following picture spread, as they feed into or were fed by many connections and spurs to and from the former British Railways system.

E.E. Class 08 0-6-0 diesel mechanical shunter #08.718 'parks' a pair of 20-ton unfitted grain wagons near the site of the former Partick West station on the short spur from the Clyde Navigation Trust Meadowside granary in April 1976. This traffic in imported grain to the Hiram Walker distillery in Dumbarton was the last rail-borne grain from this source and ceased later that year.

Geo C. O'Hara

E.E. Class 37 Co-Co diesel electric #37.149 shunts a lengthy rake of air braked cartic wagons laden with new cars at the former Elderslie car terminal in July 1984.

Tom. H. Noble

B.R.C.W. Class 26 Bo-Bo diesel electric #26.031 shunts a rake of air braked international Cargowaggon ferry vans laden with export scotch whisky from the Hill Street plant of Johnny Walker, Kilmarnock in November 1987.

Geo. C. O'Hara

B.R.C.W. Class 26 Bo-Bo diesel electric #26.014 hauls a short rake of fuel oil tank wagons along the rump of the former Port Road between Dumfries and Stranraer, bound for the I.C.I. Cargenbridge chemical complex in September 1986.

Geo. C. O'Hara

B.R. STD Class 2 2-6-0 #78026 shunts some light traffic for the mill at Garlieston on the Isle of Whithorn branch watched by a few lads and lassies on holiday from school in July 1964.

Courtesy G.N.S.R.A. Collection

Ex L.M.S.R. CRAB 2-6-0 #42908 leaves the N.C.B. sidings at Bargany Mine in the Girvan Valley, Ayrshire with a load of washed and graded coal for Ayr harbour in April 1966, shortly before closure of the southern part of the Ayrshire coalfield.

Derek Cross (Courtesy David M. Cross)

Unidentified blue liveried **CLAYTON Class 17 Bo-Bo diesel electric** brings the first train of carflat wagons loaded with vehicle products from the former B.L.M.C. plant on the Crofthead branch, West Lothian in May 1970.

David C. Smith

B.R.C.W. Class 26 Bo-Bo diesel electric #26.007 resplendent in coal sector livery pulls a lengthy rake of empty coal slurry box wagons (ex former vacuum fitted iron-ore tipplers) away from the S.S.E.B. Methil power station on the Methil branch in November 1988. This traffic emanated from Killoch Colliery washery in Ayrshire.

Geo. C. O'Hara

Unidentified **W.D. AUSTERITY 0-6-0 TANK** shunts a rake of B.R. 16-ton mineral wagons at Wellesley top, N.C.B. washing and grading sidings in March 1970. This once extensive colliery at Methil later became a site famous for the construction of jackets, decks and modules for the North Sea oil and gas industry.

David C. Smith

Ex L.N.E.R. B1 4-6-0 #61407 shunts the extensive sidings at the former showpiece N.C.B. Seafield Colliery, Kirkcaldy in September 1966. In the foreground is the track of the main line from Edinburgh to Dundee via both the Forth and Tay bridges.

Hugh Morton

N.C.B. 0-6-0 Industrial shunter #7 makes heavy work of shunting several B.R. 16-ton mineral wagons at the N.C.B. Rexco smokeless fuel plant adjacent to Comrie Colliery, Fife in October 1969.

David C. Smith

Above: **EX L.N.E.R. J38 0-6-0 #65929** comes off the short spur to the N.C.B. Dollar mine Clackmannanshire onto the rump of the former Devon Valley Branch Line with a load of coal for Kincardine Power Station via Alloa yard in June 1966.

David C. Smith

Above: Unidentified **N.C.B. 0-4-0ST Industrial shunter** marshalls a rake of loaded coal hoppers at Manor Powis Mine, near Stirling in March 1973.

Robin Nelson

Left: **B.R.C.W. Class 27 Bo-Bo diesel electric #27.025** runs wrong line towards Plean Junction, Cowie prior to reversing into the Redland Tile Co siding in December 1984. The tall signal box used to control a lengthy branch which went off to the right and served the former N.C.B. Plean Colliery which closed in the early 1960's.

Tom. H. Noble

Below left: Unidentified **E.E. Class 08 0-6-0 diesel mechanical shunter** in charge of a trip working from Perth yard is seen at the former Royal Navy stores sidings at Almondbank on the Perth to Crieff line in May 1966.

John Spencer Gilks

Below: Unidentified **B.R. SULZER Class 24 and B.R.C.W. Class 26 Bo-Bo diesel electrics** run round their trainload of steel pipes at Maud Junction yard in August 1975. This location was the nearest railhead to the site of the extensive St. Fergus gas plant following the closure of the Peterhead branch in 1970.

Courtesy G.N.S.R.A. Collection

Section 8

SELECTION OF SCOTTISH MIXED TRAIN FORMATION WORKINGS

This section of the book represents a once common type of railway operating formation that took place throughout most of the former B.R. Scottish Region. Whilst the practice was inherited from the former constituent companies that made up British Railways, the operation of mixed train formations developed considerably in the period after W.W.II and worked quite successfully at handling reasonable amounts of mixed goods in conjunction with sparse passenger loadings over usually single track branches where the infrastructure was not in place for multi train operation. The spread of pictures in this section only covers less than 30% of the mixed train routes in the former Scottish region.

Unidentified **B.R. SULZER Class 25 Bo-Bo diesel electric** stops at Melrose on a freezing December afternoon in 1968 with a Carlisle to Edinburgh Waverley route mixed train, shortly before closure of this under valued railway.

Geo. N. Turnbull

Unidentified Ex L.N.E.R. B1 4-6-0 trundles south of St. Monance with the daily afternoon mixed train from St. Andrews to Thornton Junction in April 1965.

Roy M. Crombie

B.R. STD 4MT 2-6-4T #80126 lifts a Killin to Killin Junction mixed train up Glen Dochart with the profile of Ben Lawers prominent above a fog shrouded Loch Tay below in the spring of 1965.

Colour Rail #Sc998/unknown

Unidentified and grimy but still attractive in its two-tone green livery, **B.R. SULZER Class 24 Bo-Bo diesel electric** speeds through Luncarty with a nicely mixed parcels and perishables train from Perth to Inverness in March 1967.

Roy M. Crombie

Unidentified **Ex CALEY McINTOSH 0-4-4T** rumbles through the pastoral Perthshire countryside between Balnaguard and the station at Ballinluig Junction with an afternoon mixed train from Aberfeldy in July 1961.

John Spencer Gilks

Ex-CALEY McINTOSH 0-4-4T #55200 arrives at Aberfeldy with the afternoon mixed train from Ballinluig Junction in May 1959. Note the rakes of vans and coal wagons in the goods yard behind the station sign which is untypically not the B.R. Scottish Region shade of (Caledonian) blue

Colour Rail #Sc343/D.H. Beecroft

Unidentified **N.B.L. Class 21 Bo-Bo diesel electric** rumbles through the recently closed station at Kinaldie, west of Dyce with an Elgin to Aberdeen mixed train in June 1964.

Courtesy G.N.S.R.A. Collection

B.R. STD Class 2 2-6-0 #78052 climbs past Boyndie Bay a small inlet of the Moray Firth with a nicely mixed Banff to Tillynaught Junction working in July 1961.

John Spencer Gilks

Unidentified **B.R. SULZER Class 24 Bo-Bo diesel electric** in original BR dark green livery heads the morning Inverness to Kyle of Lochalsh mixed train near Loch Luichart in June 1967.

Roy M. Crombie

Unidentified **B.R.C.W. Class 26 Bo-Bo diesel electric** approaches Corriemullie Summit near Garve with the morning Kyle of Lochalsh to Inverness mixed train in June 1967.

Roy M. Crombie

B.R. SULZER Class 24 Bo-Bo diesel electrics #'s D5126 and D5123 leaking steam from the train heating system restart a lengthy morning Inverness to Kyle of Lochalsh mixed train away from Garve station in May 1972.

Douglas Hume

Not yet adorned with half yellow warning panels **E.E. Class 20 Bo-Bo diesel electric #D8094** displaying its Scottish Region tablet catcher recess trundles a lengthy morning Mallaig to Fort William mixed train along the side of Loch Eilt in June 1962.

Roy M. Crombie

Ex L.M.S.R. Class 5 #44702 is seen in July 1961 in charge of a Fort William to Glasgow Queen Street mixed train heading towards Tyndrum Upper. The massive conical bulk of Ben Dorain beyond dominates this location with the famous horseshoe curve at the foot of the mountain.

John Spencer Gilks

B.R.C.W. Class 27 Bo-Bo diesel electric #D5364 enters Glen Dochart, west of Crianlarich with a mid-day Oban to Glasgow mixed train in September 1964. The photographer's Triumph Herald nicely dates this picture parked on the side of the A85 road.

Roy M. Crombie

Section 9

SELECTION OF SCOTTISH RAILTOUR EXCURSIONS ON B.R. METALS

This section of the book shows a brief selection of photographs depicting in many cases the "last chance to ride and see" the rump of the by then several freight only lines which still existed in Scotland up until the late 1960's. The then B.R. Regional Scottish management who comprised several tranches of professional career railwaymen actively supported this U.K. wide practice of chartering trains which traversed almost the entire extant network usually on Saturdays thus enabling many "off the beaten track" venues to be visited and photographed prior to their ultimate demise. Some 'same' specials appear throughout this chapter on different routes showing the diverse and painstaking itinerary worked out by Scottish Regions Operational management. This effort resulted in these trains covering many route miles within each working and thus made possible the following photogrpahic memories.

A pair of **Ex-CALEY 0-6-0 TENDER LOCOMOTIVES** enact possibly the busiest scene ever performed at Millisle Junction with a pair of passing "Isle of Whithorn" railtours in April 1963.

Courtesy G.N.S.R.A. Collection

Ex CALEY 3F 0-6-0 #57689 pauses on the short Shieldhall branch in the heart of the industrial dockland of Glasgow with a Railtour special in March 1963. One of the cranes of the recently modernised Barclay Curle shipyard can be seen in the distance.

Douglas Hume

THE FORMER S.S.E.B. 0-4-0 SADDLE TANK INDUSTRIAL PUG formerly resident at nearby Yoker power station, poses for enthusiasts amid a busy Rothesay Dock during July 1972. At this time this dock was used reguarly for the transportation of iron ore and coking coal for use in the then still functioning Scottish steel making industry.

Robin Nelson

Ex CALEY 4-2-2 #123 looking very attractive in arguably the most appealing livery ever to adorn a Scottish locomotive, chuffs away from Stirling with a two coach railtour composed of a pair of ex-Caley coaches in the spring of 1963. Note the rake of cattle wagons in the adjacent siding.

Robin Nelson

Ex CALEY 3F 0-6-0T #56347 decants a large posse of enthusiasts from a railtour visiting the still functional freight only Bankfoot station in April 1962.

Roy Hamilton

Ex CALEY 4-2-2 #123 makes a photographic stop at Luib in Glen Dochart whilst working a railtour on the Callander and Oban line during snowy conditions in April 1963.

W. A. C. Smith

Ex CALEY 4-2-2 #123 and Ex N.B.R. 4-4-0 #126 Glen Douglas ease away from a colourful and busy Oban station and harbour beyond with a railtour special in May 1962.

Roy M. Crombie

Looking quite surreal in tones of pinkish snow, **B.R. STD 4MT 2-6-4T #80092** hauls a pair of ex Caley preserved coaches up the branch from Killin to Killin Junction over the A85 overbridge near Lix Toll, as part of a S.L.S./B.L.S. Railtour Special in April 1963.

Roy M. Crombie

Ex L.N.E.R. J37 0-6-0 #64618 pauses at Auchterhouse where facilities still remained for goods traffic with a S.L.S./B.L.S. railtour special on the former Dundee to Newtyle line in March 1964.

Geo. N. Turnbull

Ex L.N.E.R. J37 0-6-0 #64581 pauses at the still very active goods only branch terminus of Brechin with a railtour special in June 1962. This location is now an active site of railway heritage and preservation.

Douglas Hume

Ex L.M.S.R. 2F 0-6-0 57441 brings a railtour special into the freight only station of Kirriemuir in June 1960. The extensive facilities depict the dependence this traditional Scottish market town had on the railways for the conveyance of goods and produce.

Roy Hamilton

B.R. STD Class 4 2-6-0 #'s 76108 & 76109 both in ex-works condition pause at Grantown-on-Spey East station whilst working a circular railtour through the Spey Valley in April 1961.

Courtesy G.N.S.R.A. Collection

The still functional and amazingly tidy and vandal free goods only station at Macduff plays host to **Ex G.N.S.R. 4-4-0 #49 GORDON HIGHLANDER** in charge of a visiting railtour in June 1960.
Note the rake of 12-ton blue spot insul fish vans displaying a varied range of weathered B.R. white in the seaward siding.

Roy Hamilton

A CRAVENS Class 105 2-Car D.M.U. pauses at the freight only terminus of Alford, Aberdeenshire, with a railtour special in June 1965.

Roy Hamilton

ANDREW BARCLAY Class 06 0-4-0 diesel mechanical shunter #D2420 threads the cobble inlaid quayside of Aberdeen harbour with a railtour brake van special in November 1967.

D. E. D. Blades

Section 10

SELECTION OF SCOTTISH DOCKS, PORTS AND HARBOUR RAILWAYS

This section of the book attempts to show a small number of the former nationwide railway network which was once connected to virtually every Scottish trading port. Irrespective of these location's operational function, whether they landed imported or loaded exported goods, they were rail connected and as such were responsible for a diverse range of railway traffic workings from light engine to trip, block, bulk and special wagon or full trainloads. The brief spread of pictures tries to show some of this former core railway activity.

Right:
An unidentified **E.E. Class 08 0-6-0 mechanical shunter** propels a rake of empty vacuum fitted iron-ore hopper wagons towards the massive loading tower at the former General Terminus Quay in the heart of Glasgow during April 1978. This facility along with Rothesay Dock at Clydebank became redundant after the opening of Hunterston B.S.C. deep water berth in 1980.

Geo. C. O'Hara

Left:
A panoramic view of part of the former extensive Rothesay Dock railway sidings showing **E.E. Class 08 0-6-0 diesel mechanical shunter #08.719** along with rakes of 16-ton and 24½-ton mineral wagons waiting to be loaded with imported coking coal in December 1977. Noticeable in this misty view of the River Clyde beyond are the chain driven Renfrew Ferry and the cranes of the Yarrow shipyard.

Geo. C. O'Hara

E.E. Class 08 0-6-0 diesel mechanical shunter #08.718 trundles the daily trip freight from Partick Central to Yoker yard past the dilapidated and overgrown site of Whiteinch Riverside station in January 1978. Noticeable in this view are the cranes of what were British Shipbuilders Ltd, Scotstoun Marine shipyard and North British Engine Works, both former rail connected establishments, whose tracks were severed in the 1960's.

Geo. C. O'Hara

E.E. Class 08 0-6-0 diesel mechanical shunter #08.718 propells a Partick Central to Yoker yard trip freight past the C.N.T. cranes of Meadowside Quay in the heart of Glasgow in June 1976. The larger cranes beyond served Govan Shipbuilders, Govan shipyard which lost its rail connection via the Glasgow Corporation tramway system in 1966.

Geo. C. O'Hara

B.R. STD 4MT 2-6-4T #80057 and B.R. STD Class 4 2-6-0 #76091 stand at Renfrew Wharf station with once ubiquitous workmens trains in May 1963. The rusty lines to the left led into the recently closed world-famous dredger building shipyard of Simons Lobnitz Ltd and the red brick building on the other side of the River Clyde was the S.S.E.B. Yoker coal fired power station.

Roy M. Crombie

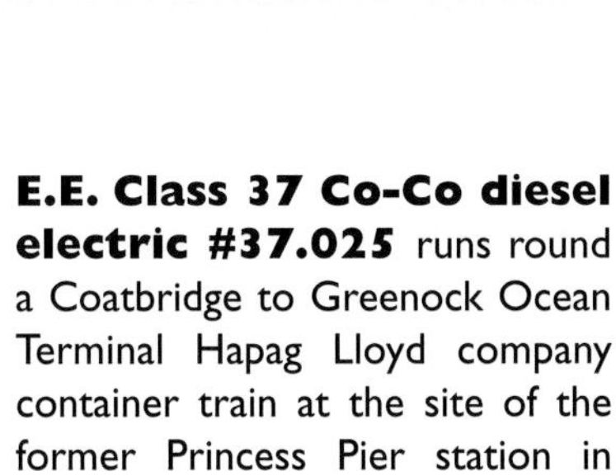

E.E. Class 37 Co-Co #37.263 trundles a trip working of loaded molasses tanks away from the United Molasses siding at James Watt Dock, Greenock bound for Mossend yard in October 1987. Note the presence of the then worlds largest self-propelled semi-submersible drilling rig 'Ocean Alliance' at the quayside of the Scott Lithgow shipyard beyond.

Geo. C. O'Hara

E.E. Class 37 Co-Co diesel electric #37.025 runs round a Coatbridge to Greenock Ocean Terminal Hapag Lloyd company container train at the site of the former Princess Pier station in March 1987.

Geo. C. O'Hara

Ex L.M.S.R. CRAB 2-6-0 #42795 marshalls a train of empty mainly unfitted 16-ton mineral wagons away from Ayr harbour coaling berths in September 1966, bound for either nearby Falkland yard or some of the then extant Ayrshire collieries.

David C. Smith

E.E. Class 20 Bo-Bo diesel electric #20.127 pulls a rake of depressed centre air braked 'Presflo' powder tanks loaded with imported cement unloaded under pressure from the adjacent coaster 'Hercules' at Ayr harbour in November 1987.

Geo. C. O'Hara

N.B.L. 0-4-0 diesel hydraulic shunter #D2718 runs down the short branch to Alloa harbour with a trip working from Alloa yard in April 1965. The tracks on the left led to Stirling via nearby Alloa marshalling yard.

David C. Smith

E.E. Class 08 0-6-0 diesel mechanical shunter #08.421 shunts a rake of imported coal in air braked HAA wagons bound for nearby coal-fired Cockenzie power station at Leith South in July 1986.

Geo. C. O'Hara

The following two sets of two pictures depict the same locomotives working at the port of Leith

Ex W.D. 2-10-0 #90773 approaches Leith docks with a trainload of coal from one of the Lothians' collieries in 16-ton unfitted mineral wagons during August 1962.

Roy M. Crombie

Ex W.D. 2-10-0 #90773 leaves the docks complex at Seafield, Leith with a long rake of 16-ton mineral wagons, probably for storage prior to export in August 1962.

Roy M. Crombie

With the shunting crew riding on 'their recess' behind the front buffer beam, **ANDREW BARCLAY Class 06 0-4-0 #D2435** passes alongside the rail served warehouse of The Iceland Steamship Co. at Leith docks on October 1970.

D. E. D. Blades

ANDREW BARCLAY Class 06 0-4-0 diesel mechanical shunter #D2435 trundles a rake of 13-ton vacuum fitted shoc wagons loaded with imported esparto grass for delivery to a rail connected paper mill from Leith docks in October 1970.

D. E. D. Blades

ANDREW BARCLAY Class 06 0-4-0 diesel mechanical shunter #D2442 descends the steeply graded branch to Kirkcaldy harbour between a pair of high grain silo buildings with a brake van in tow during September 1970.

W. S. Sellar

ANDREW BARCLAY Class 06 0-4-0 diesel mechanical shunter #D2416 shunts a couple of unfitted bitumen tank wagons along part of the Dundee Harbour quayside in August 1972.

K. G. Jones/G.N.S.R.A.

Ex L.N.E.R. Z4 MANNING WARDLE 0-4-2T #68191 propels two unfitted tank wagons along the Aberdeen Harbour quayside in May 1955. Note the masts of the then large Aberdeen trawler fleet in the distance.

Colour Rail #Sc115/J. F. Henton

E.E. Class 08 0-6-0 diesel mechanical shunter #08.855 shunts some air braked calcium carbonate powder tank wagons in Waterloo Goods yard adjacent to the Aberdeen harbour railway system in October 1990.

Geo. C. O'Hara

Section 11

SELECTION OF SCOTTISH BANKER LOCOMOTIVE ACTIVITY

This section of the book has only managed to depict four pictures showing banking assistance to train locomotives on the former B.R. Scottish Region. Nevertheless the practice of rear end assistance was necessary throughout the existence of steeply graded routes up until their closure or the advent of more powerful locomotives.

B.R. STD Class 2 2-6-0 #78050 wheezes as it banks a trainload of empty 16-ton mineral wagons from Morningside to Kingshill Colliery, Shotts in January 1963.

W. A. C. Smith

Unidentified **Ex L.M.S.R. Class 5 4-6-0** banks a nicely mixed northbound freight on Beatock bank, where the train locomotive is an unidentified **E.E. Class 20 Bo-Bo diesel electric.**

Alan Carlaw

A pair of **Ex L.N.E.R. J37 0-6-0's** lead by **#64597** banked by **#64608** haul a lengthy mixed freight through the Dundee suburb of Lochee bound for Maryfield in February 1965.

Hugh Morton

Ex L.N.E.R. J37 0-6-0 #64547 banked by an unidentified **E.E. Class 08 0-6-0 Diesel Mechanical shunter** for adhesion purposes approaches Johnshaven on the Inverbervie branch with a special in May 1966.

Roy Hamilton

Section 12

SELECTION OF SCOTTISH JUNCTIONS, SIGNAL BOXES & GANTRIES

This section of the book shows a small number of typical railway junctions, which existed throughout Scotland under the aegis of British Railways. The spread of railway junctions represented by the following photographs, depict a wide range of complicated and simple trackwork, brick and timber signal boxes and wide span signal gantries and single post signal systems as well as junctions controlled by ground frames or remote signalling centres.

Unusual motive power in the form of a pair of **E.E. Class 20 Bo-Bo diesel electrics #'s 20.199 & 20.114** in charge of a Greenock Ocean Terminal to Coatbridge Freightliner Terminal empty container train in March 1986 pass the site of the former Lyndeoch Junction, Greenock which carried the former G.S.W.R. Prince's Pier line towards Kilmalcolm.

Geo. C. O'Hara

E.E. Class 08 0-6-0 diesel mechanical shunter #08.718 takes the recently completed chord at Dalmuir Junction, Clydebank onto the re-activated Dalmuir branch with a mixed trip freight from Yoker Yard in June 1977.

Geo. C. O'Hara

E.E. Class 08 0-6-0 diesel mechanical shunter #08.719 approaches the site of the former Scotstoun West Junction with a short trip freight for Partick Central in June 1976.

Geo. O'Hara

A pair of unidentified **E.E. Class 20 Bo-Bo diesel electrics** rumble past Muirhouse Junction with a trainload of imported iron ore from General Terminus Quay to B.S.C. Ravenscraig in bottom discharge vacuum fitted 35-ton hopper wagons during November 1977.

Geo. C. O'Hara

Above:
In an urban railway scene of old industrial Glasgow, **B.R. STD Class 5 4-6-0 #73076** approaches Partick West Junction with a Rutherglen to Possil train in April 1964. Note the rakes of empty 20-ton unfitted bulk grain wagons beyond the last carriage, and the street level junction to the Clydeside Tramway to the right of the locomotive. In the distance to the right are the cranes of the recently closed Govan shipyard of Harland & Wolff Ltd.

Roy M. Crombie

Above:
A Hybrid **4-Car D.M.U. LED BY A CRAVENS Class 105 2-Car unit** passes the site of the former Blackwood Junction with a Coalburn to Glasgow Central working in February 1963. The trackbed on the left led to Hamilton via Tillietudlem.

R. M. Crombie

Right:
Stonehouse Junction in October 1964 with **CRAVENS Class 105 D.M.U.'s** at the station with trains for Coalburn and Strathaven respectively.

R. M. Crombie

Left:
Ex CALEY 3F 0-6-0 #57568 approaches Lanridge Junction with a trip freight from Chapelhall to Mossend Yard in February 1963.

Douglas Hume

Below:
A pair of **Ex-CALEY 3F 0-6-0's** presumably the famous 'twins' from Ayr shed prepare to leave Belston Junction with a loaded coal train from Littlemill Colliery bound for Ayr harbour in June 1963.

Derek Cross (Courtesy David M. Cross)

Below:

E.E. Class 37 Co-Co diesel electrics #'s 37.671 & 37.672 race past the site of Annbank Junction where the short branch to Killoch washery diverges to the left with the recently installed "silver bullet" company train from Irvine to Burngullow conveying empty china clay tank wagons in July 1990. The outline of the island of Arran is seen in the Firth of Clyde in the distance.

Geo. C. O'Hara

Ex L.N.E.R. B1 4-6-0 #61076 pilots unidentified ex L.N.E.R. V2 2-6-2 into Riccarton Junction on the Waverley Route with a southbound cement train from Dunbar in July 1966.

Colour Rail #Sc315/G.W. Parry Collection

A GLOUCESTER Class 100 2-Car D.M.U. arrives at Kilnknowe Junction, Galashiels on the Waverley route with a service from Edinburgh via Peebles in February 1962.

Roy M. Crombie

CLAYTON Class 17 Bo-Bo diesel electric #D8585 approaches Portobello East Junction with a rake of Leith General Warehouse private owner wooden unfitted grain wagons in August 1964.

Colour Rail #DE1449/Geo. M. Staddon

Drem Junction, East Lothian in June 1968, with a **GLOUCESTER Class 100 2-Car D.M.U.** on a service from North Berwick to Edinburgh about to rejoin the east coast main line more than two decades before this route was electrified.

Geo. N. Turnbull

Longniddry Junction in September 1968 with on view **GLOUCESTER Class 100 2-Car D.M.U.'s** on trains to North Berwick and Edinburgh respectively at the main line platforms and an unidentified **CLAYTON Class 17 Bo-Bo diesel electric** in the bay with the Haddington branch freight.

Geo. N.Turnbull

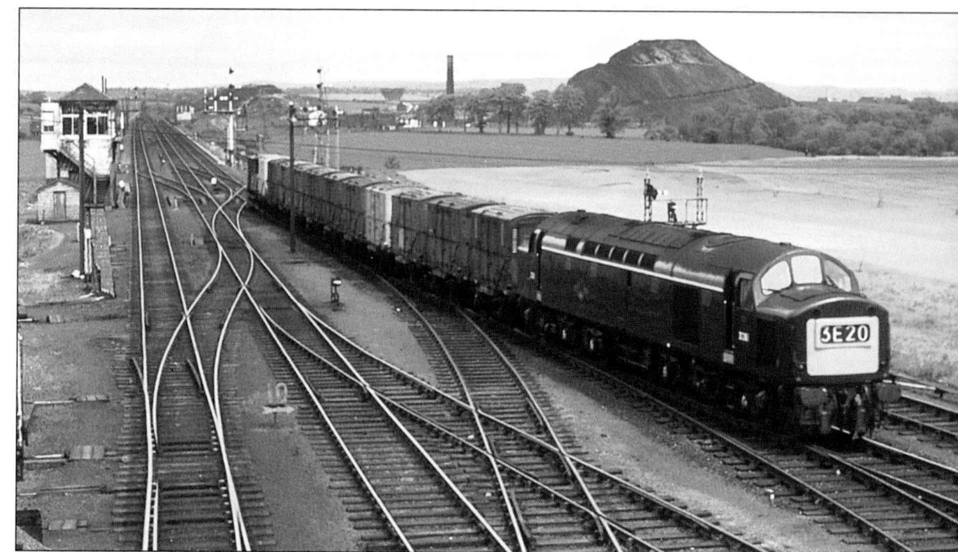

E.E. Class 40 1 Co-Co 1 diesel electric #D261 passes Thornton Junction with a train of vacuum fitted conflats conveying fish and meat in insulated containers in May 1963. Spoil heaps and pit-head architecture is still in evidence at this former area of mining in the Fife coalfield.

Ken Nuttall

Lumphinnans Central Junction in April 1964 with a **METRO CAMMELL Class 101 3-Car D.M.U.** on a service between Edinburgh and Perth passing a rake of laden wooden bodied coal wagons at this former centre of the Fife coalfield.

Douglas Hume

Ex L.N.E.R. J38 0-6-0 #65912 with steam to spare takes the line to Kincardine Power station at Kincardine Junction with a trip working comprising a load of power station coal from Alloa yard in October 1966.

Colour Rail #Sc736l
Geo. M. Staddon

A METRO CAMMEL Class 101 D.M.U. crosses over Devon Valley Junction at Alloa station with a Stirling to Edinburgh via Dunfermline service in April 1968. This station location, long since demolished, figures prominently in the much mooted project to restore railway services to this town.

Roy M. Crombie

A pair of **N.B.L. Class 21 Bo-Bo diesel electrics #'s D6109 & D6110** approach Crianlarich East Junction with a lengthy Oban to Glasgow and Edinburgh train in typical West Highland pouring rain in June 1961.

Roy M. Crombie

Ex L.M.S.R. Class 5 4-6-0 #44704 shrouded in steam at Methven Junction with a Perth to Crieff pick-up goods working in February 1963. The train is stationed on the line towards Crieff with the short branch to Methven leading off to the right.

Courtesy G.N.S.R.A. Collection

Unidentified **B.R. SULZER Class 25 Bo-Bo diesel electric** sporting a 9PO4 headcode approaches the much contracted and dilapidated Stanley Junction and the Highland main line with a return trip freight from Forfar to Perth yard in August 1975.

Ronnie Provan

Ex L.M.S.R. Class 5 4-6-0 #45461 at Kirriemuir Junction on the former Strathmore main line with a trip freight from Kirriemuir to Forfar in June 1963.

Douglas Paul

Left:
Ex L.N.E.R. J37 0-6-0 #64620 with a trip freight fom Montrose to Brechin at Dubton Junction, Angus in January 1963.

Douglas Paul

Below:
Ex L.N.E.R. J37 0-6-0 #64587 with a trip freight from Montrose to Inverbervie at Broomfield Junction in April 1963.

Douglas Paul

Below:

A pair of **N.B.L. Class 21 Bo-Bo diesel electrics** wait at the immaculate former GNSR station of Maud Junction, with trains from Peterhead on the right and Fraserburgh on the left during September 1963.

Douglas Hume

Unidentified **E.E. Class 08 0-6-0 diesel mechanical shunter** threads the pointwork at Inveramsay Junction with a trip working from Turriff to Inverurie in November 1965.

Courtesy G.N.S.R.A. Collection

B.R.C.W. Class 26 Bo-Bo diesel electric #D5346 shunts the "coast route section" at Cairnie Junction whilst at the station **B.R. Sulzer Class 24 Bo-Bo diesel electric #D5069** waits with the "glen section" of respective Aberdeen bound trains in July 1967.

Roy Hamilton

N.B.L. Class 21 Bo-Bo diesel electric #D6153 arrives at Tillynaught Junction, Banffshire with an Elgin to Aberdeen via Buckie 'coast route' train in June 1965. The platform on the right was where the train for Banff arrived and departed up until withdrawal of passenger services in 1964.

Roy M. Crombie

A CRAVENS Class 105 2-Car D.M.U. passes the still open (for freight only) Lossie Junction with a Buckie to Elgin local working in June 1965. The 'coast route' diverged to the right and the short branch to Lossiemouth headed off to the left.

Roy M. Crombie

Left:
The former H.R. station at Keith Junction in February 1963 with a then ubiquitous **B.R. SWINDON BUILT Class 120 D.M.U.** on a service to Aberdeen from Elgin via Craigellachie.

Courtesy G.N.S.R.A. Collection

Below left:
Unidentified **B.R.C.W. Class 26 Bo-Bo diesel electric** and a basic Elgin to Aviemore service at Craigellachie in June 1965. The footbridge over the line via Rothes can be seen to the left of the station buildings.

Roy. M. Crombie

Above:
A CRAVENS Class 105 2-Car D.M.U. splutters away from the junction at Craigellachie (then cut back to the coal depot at Aberlour) with an Elgin bound service in April 1968.

K. G. Jones, G.N.S.R.A. Collection

Left:
Ex L.M.S.R. FAIRBURN 4MT 2-6-4T #42269 takes the old H.R. main line at Boat of Garten Junction with an Aviemore to Forres local working in August 1957.

Colour Rail #SC1084/D. A. Kelso

Ex H.R. DRUMMOND 0-4-4T #55053 shunts a rake of wagons on the Dornoch line sidings at Mound Junction. These wagons have recently been uncoupled from the evening mixed train on the short branch from the far north line in July 1955.

Colour Rail #SC350/T. J. Edgington

Section 13

SELECTION OF SCOTTISH RAILBUS SERVICES (STEAM AND DIESEL)

This section of the book depicts a reasonably comprehensive selection of the main railbus services which were run by the former B.R. Scottish Region. The moniker railbus invariably meant a diesel railbus of the four wheel type, but the unreliability of these vehicles frequently led to their substitution by a steam or diesel locomotive hauling a corridor or non-corridor brake coach with luggage space. Most of the consists mentioned above are shown photographically in this chapter.

These three views show railbus activity on the former Lugton-Beith branch. One of the first routes to go over to four wheel diesel railbus operation, and one of the first lines to close in the early 1960's prior to the implementation of the report by Lord Beeching. The same vehicle BRISTOL / ECW #SC79958 appears on all three views.

4-WHEEL DIESEL RAILBUS #SC79958 at Barrmill station with a service from Beith to Lugton in September 1962.

Douglas Dume

BRISTOL / ECW 4-WHEEL RAILBUS #SC79958 makes the last journey from Lugton to Beith on 3rd November 1962 and is seen at the intermediate station of Barrmill.

Roy M. Crombie

BRISTOL / ECW 4-WHEEL RAILBUS #SC79958 leaves Beith station on the last train service from Beith to Lugton on 3rd November 1962. This sparsley used branch took passengers from the town of Beith adjacent to the GSWR main Ayr to Glasgow line to the isolated junction of Lugton on the GSWR main line between Glasgow and Kilmarnock, where the connecting services were less convenient, and was a closure that was not contested.

Roy M. Crombie

B.R. STD 4MT 2-6-4T #80077 near Newmilns in the Irvine valley with a Darvel to Kilmarnock railbus service in April 1964, the last year of operation of the Branch.

Roy Hamilton

PARK ROYAL BUILT 4-WHEEL RAILBUS #SC79972 near Alloway in August 1964 on the Heads of Ayr branch with a train from the Butlins Holiday Camp, the then terminus of this former line from Ayr to Girvan via Maidens.

Geo. N. Turnbull

This hastily composed picture taken from the side of the A85 road unfortunately fails to capture the grandeur of scenery and mountainous majesty of central Perthshire. **B.R. 4MT 2-6-4T #80093** is seen near Lix Toll rolling down from Killin Junction with the early morning railbus service to Killin in August 1965.

Geo. N. Turnbull

A Crieff to Gleneagles railbus service provided by an unidentified **D. WICKHAM 4-WHEEL RAILBUS** approaches the wayside station at Highlandman in February 1963.

Courtesy G.N.S.R.A. Collection

An unidentified **PARK ROYAL 4-WHEEL RAILBUS** arrives at the extensive junction trackwork at Crieff signalbox, where the driver and signalman exchange tokens prior to the short run into Crieff station with a service from Gleneagles in June 1964.

Roy M. Crombie

An unidentified **PARK ROYAL 4-WHEEL RAILBUS** leaves Muthill with a well patronised Gleneagles to Crieff and Comrie service in June 1964, shortly before closure of this branch line.

Courtesy G.N.S.R.A. Collection

B.R. SULZER Class 24 Bo-Bo diesel electric #D5122 is seen west of Grandtully with an afternoon Ballinluig to Aberfeldy railbus service in April 1965. The infant River Tay can be seen beyond the field in the centre.

Roy M. Crombie

B.R. STD 4MT 2-6-4T #80092 west of Crook of Devon with a Kinross to Stirling railbus service threading through the picturesque Devon Valley Line in April 1960.

Roy M. Crombie

D. WICKHAM 4-WHEEL RAILBUS #SC79969 in charge of a railbus service from Stirling approaches Dollar station, Clackmannanshire with an afternoon working in April 1960.

Roy M. Crombie

B.R.C.W. Class 26 Bo-Bo diesel electric #D5336 north of Grantown on Spey East amidst the forested riverbanks symptomatic of this region with a one coach railbus service from Aviemore to Elgin in June 1965.

Roy M. Crombie

Unidentified **B.R.C.W. Class 26 Bo-Bo diesel electric** and a one coach Elgin to Aviemore railbus cross over with the 10.10 ex Aviemore-Spey Valley goods train at Aberlour in June 1965.

Roy M. Crombie

PARK ROYAL 4-WHEEL RAILBUS #SC79964 at Cromdale station in the Spey Valley with a Keith Junction to Aviemore service in June 1965. Note the rake of wagons for Cromdale distillery in the siding to the right, and the neatly attended allotments next to the track.

Roy M. Crombie

Above:
B.R.C.W. Class 26 Bo-Bo diesel electric #D5345 sporting snow ploughs synonymous with B.R. Scottish Region locomotives pauses at the ornate station of Grantown on Spey West in charge of a one coach railbus service from Aviemore to Forres in February 1963.

Courtesy G.N.S.R.A. Collection

Right:
A CRAVENS Class 105 2 Car D.M.U. crosses Fraserburgh golf course with the morning railbus service from Fraserburgh to St. Combs in August 1960.

Roy Hamilton

Section 14

SELECTION OF SCOTTISH MISCELLANEOUS RAILWAY SCENES

This section of the book is a potpourri of Scottish railway scenes within the era of British Railways ownership, and whose subject matter wasn't apposite to the previous sections. Because of this the spectrum of photographs is diverse both in terms of types of trains portrayed, and variety of locations depicted, all in all a further batch of pictures showing scenes of since departed modes of British railway operating practices.

These three views on this page show scenes of street level railway operation on the former Clydeside tramway. This was an intensive system of railway sidings and yards that were connected to every heavy engineering company and shipyard at the north bank of the River Clyde between the Glasgow districts of Partick and Yoker.

Whiteinch Riverside station in September 1963 with unidentfied **B.R. STD Class 4 2-6-0 MOGUL** in charge of a Westbound passenger train. Whilst below on South Street on the Clydeside tramway an unidentified **N.B.L. 0-4-0 diesel hydraulic shunter** trundles a rake of empty bulk grain wagons towards Meadowside Granary. At this time the traffic carried on this street level system included "steel, coal, cattle, scrap metal, grain, general goods, and specials."

Roy M. Crombie

Right:
Traffic is impeded on South Street, Whiteinch Glasgow as **ANDREW BARCLAY Class 06 0-4-0 diesel mechanical shunter #D2432** trundles a rake of empty plate, bogie plate and mineral wagons from the former U.C.S. Scotstoun Division shipyard back to Yoker yard via Partick in Nov 1969. This longer route was then necessary following the removal of the west end of the Clydeside tramway system in the previous year.

W. Stuart Sellar

Left:
The view shows the same train still impeding the rapid progress of some dated 1960's style road vehicles at Partick West, where the Clydeside tramway connected to the national railway network. The street level railway crossing in the foreground led to the then active C.N.T. Meadowside Granary.

W. Stuart Sellar

E.E. Class 08 0-6-0 diesel mechanical shunter #08.718 crosses Whiteinch viaduct with a daily Partick Central to Yoker yard trip freight in November 1977. By the time of this photograph the only traffic remaining on this short branch was domestic fuel oil, coal and scrap metal. The cranes of Govan Shipbuilders Ltd distant shipyard provide a truly industrial background to this scene.

Geo. C. O'Harra

A pair of unidentified **EX L.M.S.R. Class 8f 2-8-0's** trundle past Mount Vernon in the east end of Glasgow. The working is a General Terminus to Colvilles Ravenscraig steel works trainload of imported iron-ore in a rake of vacuum fitted 25½-ton bottom discharge ore wagons in March 1961.

Roy M. Crombie

B.R. STD Class 5 4-6-0 #73072 heads towards the turntable at Gourock in March 1966. Steam working on this Glasgow south bank commuter line ended shortly after this scene, as is evinced by the profusion of overhead electrical equipment.

Douglas Hume

B.R. STD Class 9f 2-10-0 #92017 makes a 'scoop' for the photographer as it works a Larbert to Wallerscote I.C.I. Soda ash empty working in July 1967. This class of locomotive did work regularly into Scotland from Carlisle Kingmoor shed up until the end of steam facilities on B.R. Scottish Region.

David C. Smith

Ex L.M.S.R. Class 5 4-6-0 #44796 blasts almost effortlessly through Glen Ogle towards the track summit at Glenoglehead with a Glasgow Buchanan Street to Oban train in July 1961.

John Spencer Gilks

Ex W.D. 2-10-0 #90773 trundles towards the junction at Baillyfield, Leith with a lengthy rake of unfitted 16-ton mineral wagons in August 1962.

Colour Rail #Sc1078/K. M. Falconer

A pair of **N.B.L. 0-4-0 diesel hydraulic shunters #'s D2716 & D2718** repose at Alloa in April 1965, during the transition period from steam to diesel working on B.R. Scottish region. These handsome little locos would all be gone from B.R. ownership by the next decade.

Colour Rail #Sc1078/K. M. Falconer

B.R.C.W. Class 26 Bo-Bo diesel electric #26.004 hauls a trip freight from the overgrown site that was once Alloa yard back to Grangemouth in July 1986. The empty wagons in the consist conveyed molasses and grain, traffics later abandoned by Speedlink due to government edicts on remunerative rates of return on the services provided.

Geo. C. O'Hara

With some steam to spare **Ex L.N.E.R. J37 0-6-0 #64618** drifts through Lochgelly, with an eastbound train from the Fife coalfield in an azure summer day in May 1966. Note the un-vandalised ornate station lamp post.

David C. Smith

Framed by the goods yard loading gauge, a double-headed combination of different types of **Bo-Bo diesel electrics** pass Milnathort with a late afternoon Inverness to Edinburgh service in January 1970. **Class 24 #D5130 and Class 26 D5343** head this train shortly before closure of the Glenfarg route which connected Perth directly with the county of Fife.

Douglas Hume

Ex L.N.E.R. J37 0-6-0 #64618 trundles a loaded coal train from Seafield Colliery, Kirkcaldy to Thornton yard past Dysart in September 1966 with the Firth of Forth prominent beyond.

Hugh Morton

Ex L.M.S.R. Class 5 4-6-0 #45364 leaves Hilton Junction, south of Perth with an afternoon southbound west coast route parcels train in February 1965.

Hugh Morton

Unidentified **Ex L.N.E.R. V2 2-6-2** approaches the west end of Dundee with a mixed freight from the south in November 1965.

Hugh Morton

Ex L.N.E.R. J37 0-6-0 #64577 performs distant shunting duties at the freight only location of Edzell, Angus whilst working the daily trip from Brechin in May 1964.

John Spencer Gilks

A pair of scrubbed up yet unidentified **Ex L.N.E.R. B1 4-6-0's** ease through Banchory with a train of empty 'Royal stock" having conveyed H. M. the Queen to Ballater (for Braemar) in September 1962.

Courtesy G.N.S.R.A. Collection

B.R.C.W. Class 26 Bo-Bo diesel electric #D5309 pauses at Maud Junction (to clear a railtours special about to be the last passenger train to traverse the Peterhead branch) as it heads a trip freight of two 12-ton insul fish vans from Fraserburgh to Aberdeen in September 1970. Note the junction signal posts devoid of their operating arms.

D. E. D. Blades

A pair of unidentified **B.R.C.W. Class 26 Bo-Bo diesel electrics** marshall a trainload of steel pipes in vacuum fitted boplate wagons for the infant North Sea gas construction industry at Fraserburgh in the late 1970's.

W. Stuart Sellar

Unusual sighting at Forfar on the truncated remains of the former Caledonian Strathmore route between Stanley and Kinnaber Junctions. Sporting headcode **#1M35, E.E. Class 50 Co-Co diesel electric #D446** gets ready to return to Perth yard with a trip freight in April, 1970.

K. G. Jones/G.N.S.R.A. Collection

A southbound goods train headed by an unidentified **N.B.L. Class 21 Bo-Bo diesel electric** passes a northbound Edinburgh to Oban train at Glenoglehead summit crossing loop on the former Callander and Oban line in May 1964.

Geo. N. Turnbull

An unidentified **N.B.L. Class 29 Bo-Bo diesel electric** hauling a Mallaig to Fort William train consisting of multi-coloured passenger stock redolent of the transition period from British Railways to British Rail, approaches Glenfinnan station in August 1968.

Alan Carlaw

A GLOUCESTER RC&W Class 122 D.M.B.S. #SC55011 recently repainted in all over drab rail blue livery waits its next duties at Inverness station in May 1971. Several of these useful single motor brake units were used to augment the Inverness to Aberdeen express services and remained in service up until the advent of class 158 super sprinter DMU's.

Alan Carlaw

B.R.C.W. Class 26 Bo-Bo diesel electric #D5319 stops at Lairg with a once every day railway scene. The locomotive hauled far north train with Royal Mail coach in the consist is seen unloading its load of letters and parcels to an attendant Royal Mail van in May 1963.

Ken Nuttall

BRUSH Class 47 Co-Co diesel electric #47.413 makes a dusty dash past the site of the former Kittybrewster M.P.D. then converted to a depot for Aberdeen City Council, with a trip freight from Aberdeen Craiginches yard to Inverurie conveying molasses, china clay, slurry and agricultural lime (which is creating the dust) in May 1988.

Geo. C. O'Hara

Ex L.M.S.R. IVATT Class 2 2-6-0 #46460 leaves Kentallen passing a southbound goods train still in the station as it heads for Ballachullish with an afternoon train from Oban in 1962.

Roy M. Crombie

Unidentified **B.R.C.W. Class 26 & B.R. SULZER Class 25 Bo-Bo diesel electrics** pass with up and down trains at Achnasheen on the Kyle of Lochalsh line under a leaden sky in August 1967.

Geo. N. Turnbull

Unidentified **B.R.C.W. Class 27 Bo-Bo diesel electric** splutters into Tyndrum Upper with a Crianlarich Lower to Corpach company timber train during May 1975. The train consist comprises a rake of vacuum fitted Timber P wagons (re-built from plate wagons at the former B.R. Barrassie wagon works)

John Spencer Gilks

Ex L.M.S.R. CRAB 2-6-0 #42795 crosses the branch to Ayr Old Town yard with a rake of 16-ton mineral wagon empties from Ayr harbour bound for the Ayrshire coalfield in August 1966. Part of the extensive Falkland yard sidings can be seen beyond the signal box.

David C. Smith

E.E. Class 37 Co-Co diesel electric #37.517 sporting a gaudy respray colour scheme hauls an empty Stranraer to Tees Yard steel liner company working for Stockton Haulage Ltd up the Girvan Valley near Dailly in July 1990.

Geo. C. O'Hara

Unidentified **B.R. STD Class 4 2-6-0** leaves Stranraer Town with a train for Glasgow St. Enoch in April 1965. The still functional Stranraer locomotive shed (**#68C**) can be seen to reasonable effect on the right.

Robin Nelson

BRUSH Class 47 Co-Co diesel electric #47.651 heads a Glasgow Central to Carlisle local service over the former GSWR main line near Sanquar in December 1987, shortly before this service was taken over by sprinter D.M.U.'s This area of upper Nithsdale used to possess several coal mines, all of which had closed by the 1970's.

Geo. C. O'Hara

A METRO CAMMELL Class 101 3-Car D.M.U. unusually comprised of three No. motor driver units working a Glasgow Springburn to Cumbernauld service passes a derelict looking Balornock near the site of the former St. Rollox shed in November 1977. The BREL works at Springburn dominate the central background along with a cluster of Glasgow Corporation built high rise flats.

Geo. C. O'Hara

An unidentified **AL5 (Class 85) Bo-Bo electric** hauls a trainload of Linwood built Sunbeam cars past Muirhouse Junction in November 1977. This traffic ceased in the early 1980's when the Talbot car plant at Linwood closed down, thus ending Scotland's brief period as a centre for motor car manufacture.

Geo. C. O'Hara

A BRUSH Class 47 Co-Co diesel electric #47.094 hauls a lengthy nicely mixed air braked Speedlink service from Ayr yard to Carlisle south of Kilmarnock in July 1987. This train demonstrates the variety of modern wagons which were used by B.R. in the period prior to privatisation.

Geo. C. O'Hara

B.R. STD Class 3 2-6-0 #77018 a class synonymous with the short Lanark to Muirkirk route throughout their brief careers, waits in charge of a three coach train at Muirkirk station with a Lanark bound service in May 1962.

Douglas Hume

Ex L.M.S.R. Class 2 2-6-0 #46462 makes up its train at Saltoun before working back to Millerhill yard in April 1964. The author's scooter parked on the left nicely dates this composition.

Geo. N. Turnbull

A pair of unidentified **CLAYTON Class 17 Bo-Bo diesel electrics** splutter forth their unmistakeable exhaust plumes as they head a Dundee to Blackpool special bound to work south over the Waverley Route, near Millerhill in June 1966.

Geo. N. Turnbull

B.R.C.W Class 26 Bo-Bo diesel electrics #'s D5309 & D5301 hammer past Heriot with a lengthy fitted freight working on the Waverley Route in May 1963. This was a time when most of the traction on this line was still steam worked.

W. A. C. Smith

The realisation of Lord Beechings impact on the railways of Scotland is seen to good effect at the spacious layout of the former Happendon station, Lanarkshire where track lifting and other industrial vandalism is well under way on the former Lanark to Muirkirk line in April 1965. Several decades later this area is pock-marked with massive open cast coal extraction projects, and the coal is removed by giant European gauge lorries.

Roy M. Crombie

Waverley Route demoliton train comprising several bogie well wagons is seen north of Fountainhall headed by an unidentified **E.E. Class 08 0-6-0 diesel mechanical shunter** in September 1971. The partly improved A7 trunk road can be seen blasted out of the rock to the left.

Geo. N. Turnbull

N.B.L. 0-4-0 diesel hydraulic shunter #D2754 and an unidentified sister locomotive are seen in charge of the demolition train at Kelso in October 1969. The pair are probably performing their last duties before they too were consigned to be a load of scrap like the material they were recovering.

Geo. N. Turnbull

An unidentified industrial diesel shunter pauses at the picturesque Perthshire location of Strathyre station with a demolition train on the Callander and Oban line in January 1967.

D. E. D. Blades

A scene replicated throughout the entire UK railway industry in the 1950's, 60's & 70's as withdrawn steam locomotives are stored prior to being cut up for scrap. This is the McWilliam scrapyard at Shettleston, Glasgow in July 1968 with from left to right a **"JINTY", Class 5 and BRITTANIA** about to be processed. The Triumph Herald saloon belonged to the photographer and remained in his ownership for several years after this picture was taken

Roy M. Crombie

INDEX OF LOCATIONS DEPICTED IN THIS BOOK